D1445517

# THE ULTIMATE LOSS

**ALSO BY THE AUTHOR:**

*The Denim Book*

*A Motherhood Book*

*Bread*

*The Illustrated, Hassle-Free Make Your Own Clothes Book*

*Son of Hassle-Free Sewing*

*The Leathercraft Book*

*Swami Satchidananda: His Biography*

*Get Your Health Together*

*Victory Through Vegetables*

# THE ULTIMATE LOSS

## *Coping with the Death of a Child*

JOAN BORDOW

BEAUFORT BOOKS, INC.
*New York/Toronto*

155.937
B729u
c-1
12.95
8/82

*Copyright © 1982 by Joan Bordow*
*All rights reserved. No part of this publication may be reproduced or transmitted in any form or by any means, electronic or mechanical, including photocopy, recording, or any information storage or retrieval system now known or to be invented, without permission in writing from the publisher, except by a reviewer who wishes to quote brief passages in connection with a review written for inclusion in a magazine, newspaper, or broadcast.*

*Library of Congress Cataloging in Publication Data*

*Bordow, Joan Wiener, 1944-*
*The ultimate loss.*

*1. Children—Death—Psychological aspects.*
*2. Loss (Psychology) 3. Bereavement—Psychological aspects. I. Title. II. Title: Surviving the death of a child.*
*BF575.G7B67 155.9'37 81-18182*
*ISBN 0-8253-0091-6 AACR2*

*Published in the United States by Beaufort Books, Inc., New York. Published simultaneously in Canada by General Publishing Co. Limited.*

*Designer: Ellen LoGiudice*
*Printed in the U.S.A. First Edition*
*10 9 8 7 6 5 4 3 2 1*

I would like to express my great thanks to:

Mary and Andy Dinsmoor; Steve Isser; Elaine Meader; Barbara McClure; Ariel Rawhauser; Dana Silvernale; Ron Stark; and the many, many parents who anonymously shared the intimacies of their children's deaths with me.

Linda Beech; Judy Conley; Irene Ellis; Marty Enriquez; David Kaplan; Carol Kearns; Albert Knittel; Joan Lashbrook; Steven Meeks; Bob Murnane; Gail Perin; Joy Smith; and Pat Taylor, professionals who gave me their invaluable insights into their work with dying children and/or their parents; and especially to John Golenski and Stephen Levine.

Swami Satchidananda, Brother David Steindl-Rast and Rebbe Zalman Schachter.

Janet Hildebrand of the San Pablo Library for her time and patience.

Ann Overton for her feedback.

CAMBRIA COUNTY LIBRARY
JOHNSTOWN, PA. 15901

THIS BOOK IS DEDICATED TO:

*Gabrielle who provided the experience*

*Ron and Dana who provided the inspiration*

*Robert who provided the support*

*Swami Satchidananda and Werner Erhard*
*who provided the tools*

# *Introduction*

There was a time for me when birth and death were synonymous, not in an abstract or existential way, but in a very practical, experiential sense. My first child, a girl we named Gabrielle, a full-term baby, died in labor.

The doctor had hoped it was the rush of uterine blood that was blocking the fetal heart sounds. My husband held my hand and hoped. I hoped, too, but had lots of work to do and was busy with contractions and then with pushing. Also, I had the notion that babies were for being born. I had waited for this birth. I had eaten the right foods, done the right things. I deserved a baby.

The doctor performed an episiotomy and pulled her out. She was beautifully formed. I remember especially her lips; they were pursed. But she didn't move; she didn't breathe. Immediately, the doctor went to work, first massaging and then injecting her with a syringe.

There was one long moment when we heard a gurgle —maybe to be followed by a wailing sob? It passed. I sat up, stunned. We were a frozen tableau—me, my husband, a nurse on one side, the doctor bent across the table next to Gabrielle.

Someone had made a mistake. This wasn't the way it was supposed to be, the people colorless and weeping, me chopped up and numb at the same time. The doctor and my husband went off to a bar. I stayed in my bed by myself, left with the unexpected, the never spoken of. I cried till I knew I could cry forever and it wouldn't assuage the pain. I went home and sat in a chair and looked out the window into the summer streets, wondering that people could simply go about their business as if the world hadn't ended for me.

Prepared as I had been for birth, I was totally unprepared for death. There were no courses, no support groups, no reading material in 1968. People who visited didn't want to talk about it and I was afraid to bring it up. I didn't want to make them uncomfortable.

I cut my path through whatever ensued. Certain things I went through: the numbness, the disbelief, the jumbled circuitous justification and chorus of "if onlies," the burning rage and jealousy. Certain things I suppressed. They hurt too much. For instance, guilt.

I was fairly unsupported in making my way through my response to Gabrielle's death. At the same time, I was fairly unsupportable. I had begun to enjoy my role in this tragic drama and, though I would not admit it, had become reluctant to go on from there. When someone very highly regarded by me suggested it might be time for me to go on, and reached out his hand in support, my figurative response was to say, "Hand. What hand?"

I had become attached to being Rachel of the lost children, the piece of expensive crystal everyone tiptoed around. The prospect of moving out of being grief-stricken was discomforting. I had gotten used to living this way. It is not only negative changes that are uncomfortable to us humans.

Eventually, through self-observation, I realized I could live forever as the victim of a tragedy with everything that accompanies that state: sympathy, resentment, and the pain and luxury of being at the effect of my circumstances; or, I could embrace and accept what had happened—that my child was dead, that life was the way it was—and re-enter life, not as one suffering through it, surviving in spite of it, but as someone with interest in the game of life.

Later, after the death of a friend's child, I saw that one of the gifts I had been given by Gabrielle's death was that I was willing to talk about death and support the people who were left. I had been through it and so didn't fall into the trap of trying to make it different or better, of offering homilies. I didn't shun people touched by death and would allow them to go through what they needed to go through. I knew my life had actually been enhanced by my child's death. To a great extent, that is what this book is about.

*The Ultimate Loss* talks about entering into, moving through, and then going beyond a child's death through acceptance not only of what has happened but what is. It is also about choosing to live life fully, at all times, not just when things are pleasant and comfortable. It is about gathering support and contributing the insights and energy you may have been given.

In spending time with people who have integrated the death of a child into their lives in a way that enables that death to be a contribution to their lives, rather than a never-to-be-filled gap, I have observed certain components of the death-acceptance process. These will be discussed in the chapters of this book. They are:

- A choice to have the death of a child be part of life, something that happened, made a great impact (perhaps the greatest impact) in their lives, but not an event around which their lives will eternally orbit. And, a decision to live life is made.
- Permission by the parents to enter into and go through whatever needs to be experienced in resolving the death.
- Not shutting down. Continuing to communicate to others about whatever they are experiencing, no matter how painful.
- Gathering support from people who will give them permission to go through what is necessary, rather than try to stop the process with comfort.
- Contributing what they have gained and, thereby, creating a spiral effect.

When I say "accept," sometimes it is taken to mean pasting on a happy face to mask true feelings, the anger or sorrow or resentment bubbling just under the surface. I certainly do not mean this, for surely we have enough pretense in our lives already, enough armoring and covering up, enough shielding of our discomfort so we can look good at the expense of really being ourselves. I am not talking about "positive thinking" either, labeling something we think is negative as positive and then feeling better about it.

Accepting our lives the way they are requires a commitment to eliminating our pretenses, despite the brief comfort and numbness our pretenses give us. It requires us to observe how we operate, to become conscious of our actions and thoughts, to, perhaps, see ourselves as if we are other than ourselves. At some point, we must face the fact that no matter how much we resist the way our lives are and the way we are, it doesn't change things anyway. Pretending things aren't the way they are doesn't make any difference.

Although I refer to the death of a child as an opportunity, I am not saying it isn't a tragedy; it is both. Despite the opportunity, given the chance to learn the lessons inherent in a child's death in any other way, I don't know anyone who wouldn't choose another way, or choose to have the child back. However, what I'm talking about is how it is, not how we would like it to be.

# 1

A great master of Zen, as well as of *haiku* poetry, was commissioned by the head of a dynasty to write a poem that would bless and commemorate the dynasty. A few weeks later, the master returned and read the poem. It said:

*Grandfather dies*
*Father dies*
*Child dies*

The head of the dynasty was outraged. This was no blessing; it was a curse! He was about to have the master beheaded, when the latter said:

"What is a greater blessing on a house than that the oldest dies first?"

The death of a child is said to be the most devastating death. It is the one we least expect, the one we deny and fear the most. It is an affront both to our evolutionary strivings and our sense of fair play.

Just as we are supposed to outlive our parents, our children are supposed to outlive us. We regard them as the part of us that will endure, our future and our hope.

"In a symbolic, as well as a real sense," says John Golenski, chaplain of Oakland Children's Hospital, "children are our image of immortality. When a child dies it undercuts our defense system against the fact of our own mortality. Even people who don't have children are queasy about facing the death of a child."

Our children exist not merely as our children. These bodies, temperaments, personalities with particular thoughts and feelings are also a metaphor for that which is to come. Their deaths are not only felt as the absence of a particular individual but as an amputation of an essential part of ourselves, something that is gone and cannot be replaced. They leave an emptiness, a hole that seems to stretch from one end of the universe to the other and swallows up everything.

These deaths that are not supposed to happen, do happen. In the most recent statistics available, we see 137,000 people dying between the age of birth through twenty-nine. When fetal deaths are added, the figure rises by 32,000 people.*

The death of children has very little to do with what we want or do not want; like or do not like; think should or should not be. Once it happens, and we are in the middle of the experience, all our thoughts, judgments, considerations, and beliefs are like a handful of chaff in a cyclone. The full force of the situation sweeps everything

*Figures for 1978 from the 1980 Statistical Abstract of the United States, United States Department of Congress, Bureau of the Census.

before it, reducing our most precious ideals to nothing, testing everything we hold ourselves to be.

Death destroys the illusion that things are permanent, impervious to change. It takes all that we hold dear and chews it up and throws it back at us. Death tears down all our carefully constructed fortresses and leaves us naked, thrown back upon our essence alone, that fundamental nature we may never have had an opportunity to see before.

The falseness of everything we have counted on to give us pleasure, to make us happy, becomes glaringly apparent. We see that our bank balances no longer matter, that the exciting plans for the future no longer mean anything in a universe where the future cannot be a sure thing.

Death affords those who are left an opportunity to reevaluate everything. And though we would give all we have to defer that opportunity, it exists anyway. It allows us to see the flimsiness of our expectations, to realize there is no expectation without disappointment; it allows us the possibility of being more sensitive, more vulnerable, to let others support us, and to notice the integrity and love often left unobserved in life's fast pace.

Mainly, it gives us the chance to live life in the present. Most of us go through life as if we have all the time in the world, as if our bodies are immortal. Our culture, the great importance we place on our possessions and things, as opposed to relationships and intangibles, supports this illusion of permanence. Stephen Levine, a Buddhist meditation teacher as well as one of the principles in the Hanuman Foundation's Dying Project, says, without sarcasm, "Die now and avoid the June rush."

He means that if we lived our lives with the certainty of our deaths, perhaps they would become precious. We would no longer waste time and energy on attaining positions of power and money and on dominating and manipulating others, but rather would begin to place importance on transferring our love to others.

Very often, we hear the parents of children who have died express regret about not spending enough time with their child, not really telling them they loved them. They can then use this information to renew their relationship with other children, other family members. They have found there is no time *but* the present.

*DANA:*

Sean had a perfect birth. We had him at home, with a Le Boyer birth. When he came out, he went right onto my stomach. I touched his head when he was crowning and then he went onto my belly, all slippery and wet. It was at night, so the children were asleep until I started pushing and then Ron woke them to come and see him be born.

Sean was an idyllic baby. He nursed, and let the children hold him without fussing. And he was very easy to comfort for about a week. Then he started getting irritable.

One night he was screaming when I went to change him. I got a washcloth and when I returned to Sean, he was limp. I woke Ron up and we called the doctor, who said he'd have to look at him to determine what was the matter. After a lot of stimulation, he was awake enough to nurse. Then he went back to sleep until dawn. When he woke, he was limp again and I couldn't get him to respond—to cry or nurse—before he went back to sleep again. When he awoke at three in the afternoon, his breathing was irregular and his hands were beginning to turn blue so we rushed him to the hospital. He stopped breathing in the emergency room. He only missed one breath and the hospital was ready with a respirator. I was hysterical. All I could say was, "Sean, we love you so much. We don't want you to go." He seemed very peaceful, though. He didn't show any fear.

We held his hand and comforted him through all the IVs and blood tests and the strangeness of the hospital. He cried a lot but I didn't mind a bit because I was so happy he was responding again. The hospital said he had a urinary tract infection and his kidneys had shut down under the strain. They corrected his salt balance, gave him IV antibiotics, and "milkshakes" made of water, sugar, and essential fatty acids, and he started showing signs of improvement. He was really spunky and screamed and complained a lot.

They did numerous tests on him—X-rays, sonar scans; they injected dye and nuclear medicine into his veins. They never asked for our permission before running tests on him and we became very protective and demanded we be consulted before they took any more tests. When the levels of toxins in his blood and his kidney functions were safe, we took him home.

After five days, he came down with a fever. He had

gotten moniliasis in his mouth from the antibiotics and we treated it with Microstatin but it wasn't working. We took him to the hospital and I spent the night with him, but took him home when there was no change in his condition. Then he started feeding poorly because of his sore mouth and we brought him back and had him fed intravenously. His fever was a mystery no one could figure out and his white cell count was abnormally low. Sean's mouth was too sore to take a plastic nipple, so I stayed with him in the hospital to breast-feed him. When they attempted to tube-feed him, he fought it, gagged, and threw up.

At the request of our physician, we took Sean to a medical center. Our first impression of it was that this was truly a horrible place. On the pediatrics floor were many children with leukemia, walking around pushing carts with IVs hanging from them.

I needed to stay overnight to learn how to tube-feed Sean so if we took him home the next day, I could do that myself. I took over his hospital tube-feedings because the nurses couldn't keep him calm enough to hold still. The next day, we were afraid to take him home in case his condition worsened. It's funny how things change. At first we thought the hospital was hell, but after being there a while we got used to it, and we weren't willing to be responsible for taking him home and having him die.

Ron had to work and look after our other two children. I had to stay and make the decisions. I can't remember all the tests Sean had. They started out slowly and then snowballed. First one X-ray and one blood test, and then there were bone marrow tests, and more X-rays, and then dye injected into his veins. Every feeding took almost an hour. Sean wasn't getting much sleep and I wasn't getting many meals.

*RON:*

One day Dana was in the hospital with Sean and I was driving when all of a sudden, I felt as if all my energy had drained from my body. A hot rush went through me and my heart started to beat violently. I drove to a hospital because I thought I was having a heart attack. They checked me out and said I was okay. The next day, when I drove the kids to school, this anxiety started again. I began to be aware of the guilt I was feeling over the fact my son was so sick. I remembered I hadn't been very supportive of our having another baby. Even though, after his birth, that distance got blasted away. There were times I felt like saying "Fuck you," to God for creating such misery and suffering in the world, but I wouldn't let myself express that because I thought it wouldn't do much good for either me or Sean, so I tried to stay positive instead.

I called various groups of friends from different spiritual affiliations. Some I asked to chant for Sean's well-being, some I asked to pray. We were given a beautiful prayer which Dana and I did together. When I was with Sean, I would close my eyes and imagine him being enveloped in light.

*DANA:*

One afternoon, Sean was given a drug called chloral hydrate because they wanted him to hold still for an X-ray. He had had lots of bad-tasting stuff but this time, he threw back his head and screamed, as if he were saying, "NO, NO!" The next morning, an X-ray showed his ureter to be blocked in three places and moniliasis in his urine, which meant the infection was in his bladder and kidneys. He had had a second dose of chloral hydrate for the X-ray.

The staff was ecstatic, like on TV when a great medical mystery is solved. They felt now they could really do something.

But on account of the chloral hydrate, Sean was burping a lot and his stomach was very distended and filled with gas. The doctors planned to perform surgery on the blockage that night and to give him an antibiotic to kill the moniliasis. It was a drug toxic to the kidneys but the moniliasis itself was causing ulcers in the kidneys.

Sean was given a general anesthetic and underwent surgery. When he came out, his stomach was even more distended. We later found out that the anesthesia can suppress bowel movements for two days.

Sean seemed horrified by the pain he awoke with. They gave him morphine. In thirty-six hours, he had taken two doses of chloral hydrate, a general anesthetic, morphine, and a large dose of antibiotics.

I went through everything from feeling it wasn't worth it and we should quit because Sean was being tortured, to feeling elated over the fact he would now make it.

I left the hospital for a short time and when I returned the doctors were very concerned. They feared

Sean would have a cardiac arrest because his blood pressure was dropping and they wanted to know if they should put him on life support systems or let him go. I called Ron and told him he'd better come because Sean might not live through the night.

In order to do a cross-test on his blood type, the doctors needed to give Sean another blood test, which they were unable to do because the veins in Sean's heels wouldn't bleed enough to insert a needle. He needed red blood. They did an X-ray which showed his bowel was seriously distended and on the verge of rupturing. They knew then he had not been in shape for surgery but there was nothing they could do now that the surgery had been performed.

Then his tissues started to swell up with fluid. I said, "They're not going to blow you up anymore. Your belly is all blown up and now your skin is blowing up, too." I asked the doctors if they thought he would make it and they said they didn't think so. Up until that point, I had never felt he was dying, but figured he was being maintained until we could find a solution.

When the doctors asked if they should cut the tubes, Ron became very upset. He said no. He couldn't believe it was really happening.

Sean had been out of it for quite a while. His eyes were closed and it was hard to get into contact with him. I had always planned that if he were to die, he would die in my arms. So they cut all the tubes and the three of us sat down in a big chair. I held Sean in my arms and Ron put his arms around both of us. Sean opened his eyes then and looked at us. He didn't look like he was in pain anymore. Then he curled up in my arms. We talked to him. We told him what was happening, that his body just wasn't good enough for him to live in any more and that it was okay for him to go. We cried the whole time. We told him there would be no more pain and he would be loved and taken care of, that he could just relax and let go, and that it was okay. He began to breathe very hard.

Ron began chanting to him through his tears. Then Sean's breathing got more shallow and relaxed. His eyes were very dark and sparkling and clear. The lower part of his face got cold, but his cheeks were still warm. Slowly, he began to close his eyes and look at us through lowered lids. Finally, his eyes closed. His forehead remained warm and there was a red line which extended up the center of his forehead. The line slowly moved upward. The last part of him to become cool was the top of his head. His soft spot was very wide. I didn't want to put him down until I was sure he was all the way out. Then I laid his body down.

I had held this baby for the last nine days and all of a sudden I had had to put him down. My arms ached. I couldn't get home to my other children fast enough.

I picked up my seven-year-old, Cristily. We sat outside on the grass and I told her. She cried for at least twenty minutes. When she was done, I told her he had gone to the angels, that he didn't have to suffer any more, and that he was all right. Then I picked my three-year-old, Josha. He asked where Sean was. I told him Sean had died. He'd never seen death, not even the death of an animal, and I didn't know just how to explain it to him, so I asked if he remembered where he'd been before he came into my tummy. He looked off, seemed to see something, and said, "Yes." I said, "Well, that's where Sean is. He's left his body and gone off with the angels." Then he cried, and later said he saw Sean going through the forest near us.

The first night after Sean died, I put off going to bed until late. I was exhausted but I was afraid of having nightmares, visions of the hospital. When I finally slept, I dreamed the same dream all night. It was of Sean's body floating in midair before me with the IV tube in it. At the same time, his eyes were really dark, just the way they were before he died. He was speaking to me, telling me he was all right, that I'd done a good job, that I hadn't done anything wrong and shouldn't feel guilty. He was comforting me. In fact, he was no longer a baby and was more mature than me. That saved me a lot of mental torment. For a few days, I felt his presence very strongly. It was as if he made his adjustment very quickly and then he stayed with us awhile to make sure we adjusted also.

*RON:*

I was surprised to see how easy it was for us to have the kind of ritual we wanted. We didn't have to have our son's body embalmed and we were able to drive it with us to the cemetery. We had put his body into a wooden box with white material outside it. I dug the grave myself in a beautiful graveyard on a hill, with trees and a view of forests, the kind of graveyard where people decorate the graves with flowers and shrubs.

After I dug the grave, everyone arrived. It was one of those perfect spring days, warm, with birds chirping.

One of our friends was a minister. He had come to the house before the funeral and we had talked about how we wanted it to be.

At the funeral, we all sang "Here Comes the Sun," "Turn, Turn, Turn," "Let It Be," and "I Shall Be Released." Dana sang "Brother Sun and Sister Moon." I read St. Francis's Canticle to Brother Sun and the minister's wife read a passage from *The Jewish Book of Wisdom,* which said when a man dies at an early age it is because his life has been pleasing to God, who has taken him back so he could have fewer trials.

*DANA:*

Cristily called her teacher to tell her. The children went to a very closely-knit private school and the teachers in each grade told their classes about Sean, with a story about a little angel who had come to earth for a very short time to teach his parents something, and then went back to God. In the third grade, they learned a lullaby which they then sang to the second grade. I used to teach handwork in the school and this experience brought me much closer to all the children there.

I asked Josha if he would like us to have another baby and he said, "No, because you buried Sean." So I told him a story about some children who had found a baby bird that had fallen from its nest and broken its neck. The children tried to nurse it through the night, but in the morning it died. Then the angels came and the little bird flew out of its body into an angel's hands and they took it up to heaven where it flew among beautiful trees like clouds. The children looked into the bird's box and saw the dead body and they buried it and planted flowers over it. When the baby bird looked down from heaven and saw the flowers, it was very happy. Sometimes, it would look down on the children and sing and sing. At the part of the story where the bird died, Josha cried, but he was happy at the end. He laughed when I told him the bird was singing.

Almost everyone cried when we told them about Sean's death. That was fine with me when he first died but after a while I didn't want to think about it and cry all the time. And I couldn't stop thinking about it. So I became very busy, working in the garden incredibly hard, buying more seedlings than I could plant before they died. My work became compulsive; dinners were late because I didn't want to stop gardening. Once, while weeding raspberries, I got a thorn in my hand. It swelled up and I needed to stop working and soak it. The thorn didn't come out and I went to the hospital to have it removed and found I needed to be hospitalized. I started crying because I realized I had been avoiding dealing with my feelings over Sean's death. When they put an IV into my vein I thought that must be how it felt to Sean. Then I went into surgery and thought, that must have been as it was for Sean. When I woke up I felt as if a nail had been driven through my hand. My hand felt like Sean's whole body.

*RON:*

I found most people wanted to know about Sean's

condition while he was sick but they didn't want to hear my experience of it. I think everyone has a hard time confronting suffering and death. Our pediatrician sent us a note to express his sympathy but also to tell us he had found a lot of things that were positive about the experience, especially his warmth over having worked with us.

*DANA:*

The experience of Sean's death made Ron and me unable to tolerate the fighting we had spent a lot of time on. We were so wide open that any attack was too painful. And we became able to look at why we had been fighting instead of communicating.

Someone told us, "When someone you love dies, what you've left with is love." We both loved Sean so much, that when he died we loved each other more, and we could be more compassionate and understanding toward everyone around us.

Elisabeth Kübler-Ross and others have observed that dying people tend to go through different stages, or move through different spheres, on the way to accepting their death. These stages have been called denial (resisting the information or knowledge that one is dying); anger; bargaining (the hope that one can stave off death); depression; and acceptance, and there is disagreement about whether or not they follow one another in a specified pattern. People close to the dying person also go through similar spheres when dealing with that death. In the case of sudden, unexpected death, a progression does not seem to occur.

Dr. John Graves, writing in the Grief Education Institute's Newsletter (issue 7, February 1981), pointed out the difference between grief and what has been called both mourning and "grief work."

"Grief is a relatively short and somewhat stereotyped phenomena involving a sequence of intense feelings, thoughts, behavior and changes in body state directly following an irretrievable loss. Grief is a subcategory of an acute stress reaction in which the human organism is mobilized in both a biological and emotional sense for the task of survival and obtaining ongoing support and nurturance, in the face of the reality of death of a loved one. Mourning, on the other hand, is a complex, highly individualized and lengthy process which appears to be more socially determined, and perhaps more dependent on early life experiences than grief."

What he is pointing out is that grief is an automatic, mechanical reaction of the human organism, while mourning is related to what we do with that reaction. In grief work or mourning we can see the differences between a parent who continues to move through the tremendous disruption of his or her life and the emotional turmoil, despite the pain and discomfort, and one who remains stuck in the tragedy of the event for years; between one who integrates the death of a child into the whole of their existence and one who remains a victim of the disaster; between one who can actually transform apparent misfortune into an opportunity and a contribution, and one whose life has stopped at the moment of the child's death.

For many of us, living after the death of a child is

tough, hard work. It calls upon all of our inner resources, all of our willingness to endure at a time when it looks easier to give up, drop out of life, become insulated from the pain. It requires capabilities that may be dormant from lack of exercise. It may entail circumventing old patterns of seeking the most comfortable path at all costs. It is not easy.

Some of the grief processes' components are: shock, embarrassment, jealousy of people who have not lost their children; guilt; anger; a sense of unreality. Some parents—especially when their children have gone through a lot of physical pain before dying—will experience great relief, even euphoria, which others may view as inappropriate.

Parents may find themselves behaving in ways previously unknown to them. Forgetting their words in mid-sentence; crying at the drop of a hat; thinking they have gone crazy; and dealing with friends who think they have gone crazy are some reactions.

*MARYELLEN:*

I had an ominous feeling when Eric first started showing signs of being sick. I thought he had a flu, which lasted about a week and a half. He would come home in the afternoon from school very tired and would go to sleep. During this time, one day I was walking down the house stairs and he couldn't keep up with me. He sat down on one of the steps and screamed that I didn't care about him. He said, "I'm going to die and you don't care." At the time, it struck me with a ring of truth but I dismissed it. As Eric got sicker, I wouldn't tell anyone about this but would think about it often. I had a very strong feeling he was going to die.

It took about a month to get a diagnosis. While he was being tested to see what was wrong with him and why he continued to be so tired, it was Halloween. Eric was six and it pained him not to be able to go trick or treating. He told me, "I'll never go trick or treating again." He just wanted out of the hospital and was terrified of all the testing.

Eventually, he went in for a diagnostic operation from which he never regained consciousness. They opened him up, found inoperable cancer, and closed him back up. After that, Eric would open his eyes every so often but never seemed to know who was there. His stares were blank.

After we knew it was cancer, my sisters came and took over our household and the two other children—John, one and a half, and Stuart, eleven. They created a nice homey atmosphere but Stuart felt he didn't have us, and the whole situation was very mysterious to him. Once he visited Eric in the hospital but it was so traumatic for him he wouldn't go back again. My husband, Walt, and I were tired all the time and didn't give the kids much attention.

Walt and I traded off staying at the hospital. We would stay until 10 P.M. and return at 7 A.M. Watching Eric's physical deterioration was the hardest part and I almost felt Walt and I were doing embalming techniques with him—making sure his pillowcases were new and bright, combing his hair, washing his face, powdering him, all with no response.

I was pregnant when Eric became ill. Jennifer was

born at the same hospital Eric was staying in. Everyone came and made a big fuss over her and brought presents and flowers and said, "Isn't she beautiful!" But I left her in the care of the nurses and went downstairs to be with Eric. It wasn't that I rejected her, it was that I thought she was being taken care of and Eric wasn't. I think I made a pretense of being a cuddling mother toward Jennifer but I really wasn't. I decided not to nurse her because I didn't want to spend time on that when I needed to be with Eric.

During the time, I felt the things people talked to me about were incredibly silly and trivial. For instance, a very good friend would visit me in the hospital and tell me about how difficult it was to decorate her house properly. I felt incensed that she had the nerve to say that to me.

However, I wasn't ready to share my feelings then, even with the people whom I felt closest to. I couldn't even share things with Walt, and our relationship became very strained for a while. Though we could sense each other's feelings, we couldn't put those things into words. We've discussed those times in the years since Eric's death, but not very often.

Eric died about three weeks after Jennifer's birth and I was really lonely inside for a long, long time. For about two months I went to the cemetery every day. As far as taking care of the other kids, I did what needed to be done physically but emotionally, I removed myself. For a time, I took on Eric's symptoms. I imagined myself getting cancer, had pains in my stomach and so forth. Though I was drained, I felt a strong need to get my life back in order. I insisted we move to a new house and Walt went along with that.

My oldest son, Stuart, had shared a room with Eric. The day Eric died, Stuart cried and cried. After that, he didn't want anybody to touch his room. He would only let me go into it to make his bed and rearrange his side of it. About Eric's things, he would say, "Don't worry about that stuff. It's fine. Leave it alone." Eventually, I cleaned Eric's stuff out of the room and packed it in boxes.

The day Eric was buried, Stuart went on his paper route instead of going to the funeral. It seemed to me he was going on as he had before his brother's death, and we didn't question his behavior, even though there were small signs that all was not well with him. Six years later, it all came to a head.

By that time, Stuart had totally rejected my husband and me. The rest of the family, including the two younger children, had become objects of his hostility. Finally, in the space of a week, he put his fist through one wall, his foot through another wall, his hand through a closet door, and pushed the front windshield out of the car.

When he was around, the two little ones wouldn't leave my knees. I couldn't get a babysitter because Stuart would terrorize them, also. Finally, we all went to a family counselor.

We found out Stuart's anger stemmed from his feelings about our having spent so much time at the hospital with Eric and his thinking that this had meant we didn't love him any more.

When the counselor asked me how I had felt about the way Stuart was acting, I said, "It feels like he's died. I've finally accepted Eric's death as a reality but here I have a living, breathing son that I can't touch."

The counseling was a turning point for us. We hadn't understood what he was feeling and he hadn't known we really did love and care about him. After that, the whole atmosphere in the house changed. Stuart began acting gentler, more tolerant of everyone. He began to reach out and include us in his life again.

Linda Beech, a grief counselor, says the death of a child is the most disruptive death. "These people have turned a corner that will provide some scary places and will also open incredible vistas. They should be encouraged to cope with themselves as totally new people and to understand that probably nothing is ever going to be the same again."

Often, people report differences in the experience of a sudden death versus an anticipated death. When a child dies suddenly, there has been no time for the preparatory grief work that often accompanies a terminal illness. In such cases, grieving may begin when a prognosis of a life-threatening illness has been reported, and a level of acceptance reached by the time the child dies, especially when such a death releases the child from extremely painful circumstances.

Dr. David M. Kaplan, Ph.D., Director of the Division of Clinical Social Work at Stanford University Medical Center, speaks of the benefits of anticipating the death of a child when there is a life-threatening illness present: "In our survey, many people didn't anticipate the death when there were a hundred reasons they should have and when there were all kinds of confirmations of the bad news. While some families can take that and use it, others were totally surprised when their children died. It was like they had suddenly been in an accident.

"To be able to know and feel and act as if you are in a bad situation, to live with that, to let everyone in the family do that, and to console one another, seems to be the way to deal with this so that, in the long run, you are left with the least amount of problems. The few families in our study who did that were left with very few negative aftereffects. The people who couldn't do that were usually a mess."

John Golenski, a chaplain, says, "The common tale is that grief is easier if there is a long-term death. I don't agree. I think that the two ways are just different. A sudden death is an overwhelming shock and the biggest issue seems to be accepting the fact of death. Because of this, I think it's very important to see the body of the child. With an illness, while you have time to prepare for the death, you not only lose the child but the reason for all the activities you've been performing. In many cases, particularly with mothers, their whole life has been scheduled around the sick child: visiting, caring, and sometimes this has gone on for years. Then it all ends. Not only is the child gone but so is the meaning and structure of their life. There's a sense of open time, with nothing to do."

Sudden death by suicide is ranked as the eighth leading cause of death in people between the ages of five and fifteen; the third in the fifteen–twenty-four years old range (following accidents and homicide); and the fourth in the twenty-five–forty-four year old group.

Margaret Reilly's youngest son, Jeff, committed suicide at the age of twenty-one.

"I first noticed Jeff's social problems in grade school, as he was doing very badly. These problems became much more pronounced when he was eleven, and his dad died. When I remarried, two years later, Jeff and my other son never got along with their stepfather. I took both boys for testing in high school, to find out why their school work was going so poorly. The man who tested Jeff said it was as if he just wasn't functioning or making connections. My feeling was that he'd almost become paralyzed in his thinking. At that time, we sent both boys to private school, and the whole family went for counselling. But the situation between my husband and the boys was at a standstill. It went round and round with nothing being resolved.

"Jeff dropped out of high school before graduating, and he and his girl friend moved out of their homes and went to live in Oregon together. After two years, she left because she felt he was smothering her with his jealousy. He moved back to our area and I began to see him again.

"In 1977, he got a good job and it looked like things were finally going well for him. He told me he was going to enroll in a community college. Just before he quit his job, things took a downturn and, for the first time, I heard him mention the term 'suicide.' I later found out he had talked about this for a long time. He seemed to sink way down in his life and then manage to pull himself up, but now he was on a definite slide. When he came over and I tried to get him to talk about his problems, he would get so angry he would slam the doors till they broke.

Sometimes, he would come over and just stay out on the deck alone and pace back and forth.

"Early that July, I told my older son Don that we had to commit Jeff to a hospital for treatment, which Jeff had refused to do. I called the suicide prevention group for advice but they said they couldn't ask to speak to Jeff on the phone. He had to call them.

"I then called my psychiatrist and described how much Jeff's situation had deteriorated. He told me to bring him to the hospital and he would try to talk to him and have him agree to commit himself. I knew Jeff wouldn't go with me, so I had Don drive him there. However, there'd been a mix-up, and my psychiatrist wasn't there yet and Jeff refused to sign himself in. I persuaded the psychiatrist on duty to talk with Jeff but, after he did so for a few minutes, the doctor told me he thought Jeff was fine and should be allowed to just go on his way. Jeff hitchhiked back to his house.

"After that, I would visit him at his home but he didn't want to talk to me. After a few minutes of being polite he would always ask me to leave.

"I became more and more anxious about the situation. I was scheduled to visit my mother in Washington State and had asked Jeff to go. He considered it but then refused. Just before I left for Washington, I had asked a policeman, a classmate in a course we were both taking, to come with me to Jeff's and see if he could talk to him. We went to his house the night before I left for Washington but Jeff was not at home.

"Not knowing where he was or what I should do, I went to my mother's for the visit. Two days later, my husband called with the news: Jeff's body had been found in a remote area in his car. He had shot himself through the head.

"I went numb with shock but, having always been the type of person who had the strength to do what was needed, I became extremely active. I had to do something. I immediately returned home. I went to the Coroner's Office to see Jeff's body. 'Blond boy found dead in car' was not enough for me. I wanted to make sure it was Jeff. They had already performed the autopsy and wouldn't let me see his body. I then talked to the sheriff to find out everything he knew about Jeff's death. It was difficult and grim, of course, but I needed to do it for myself.

"For a long time I felt terribly guilty about not having been able to get Jeff to commit himself to the hospital. I went over and over in my mind all the things I could have done. Eventually, I realized I couldn't do anything but what I had done.

"I received a book, *How to Survive the Loss of A Love*, by Colgrove, Bloomfield and McWilliams, which introduced me to the grief process, adding enormous insights and understanding.

"My interpersonal relationships changed enormously. The pretense I had had that my life was always wonderful vanished. I determined it would not serve me and those I loved for me to erect those barriers again. This included a decision never to hide the fact of Jeff's suicide from others. I began to get acquainted with my relatives and friends in a new, real way. It was deeper, and a new caring and understanding occurred. Though it was very rewarding, it was not all easy. I discovered others were as resistant to being open as I had once been.

"What I learned was more and more about people and more and more about myself—the deep universalities and the surface differences.

"Jeff's death affected my whole philosophical viewpoint. I now think souls choose their parents, not the other way around. I feel Jeff is now working on his eternal soul. And I don't think you are damned if you take your own life, even though every religion says it's a no-no. God loves everybody. He just says we have to keep working on ourselves until we manifest the love we've got that we're covering up."

The idea that young children are not—or should not be—aware of death remains with us, not because it is true, but because it serves to protect adults at certain vulnerable points.

Stephen Levine, who has worked with both dying children and their parents, says: "It's very easy for children to die. They know they're not the body. I was with a two-and-a-half-year-old who was dying of leukemia in a New York hospital. As I came to the side of the crib, the child looked up at me. He didn't cursorily look into my eyes the way we usually do; he went right into my eyes and stayed there before going on to the next person. He was very present, not flitting around. Looking into his eyes was like looking into the night sky. They were wide open. He seemed to have no resistance to what was happening. Though the leukemia had wreaked havoc with his body and though the treatments produced effects which most of us would have found distracting and painful, causing most of us to go into hellish resistance to the present moment, he manifested none of that.

"Outside his room, his mother said, 'It's very strange, but it feels all right to me that my child is probably going to die. I feel confused and guilty, how could it be all right for my little boy to die? And yet that place in me keeps getting stronger and stronger and more pronounced as if I know if he dies that's exactly what is supposed to happen.'

"Originally, the boy's father insisted his son wouldn't die. The more he held on to the hope that his son would live, the more painful it was for the father. But as the boy grew closer to his approaching death, the father had an extraordinary opening up, which he couldn't understand either. He told me, 'I don't know why it's okay with me for him to die, but it is.' I saw this as being due to the child's clarity. He wasn't holding on, nor was his mother, and so it gave the father an alternative to the 'holding on' he'd been conditioned to do all his life."

Stephen Levine's experience is that the younger children are, the easier it is for them to accept their death. Since they lack a solid, substantial concept of death, they are more willing to go through the actual experience without fearing or resisting it.

This is confirmed by the Center for Attitudinal Healing in California, which includes support groups for children with life-threatening illnesses, as well as separate ones for their parents.

Within the children's groups, it has been observed that they share the possibility of their deaths in a very open way. However, they are often afraid to broach the subject with their parents, sensing they will not be willing to discuss it.

When children and parents first come to the center, they are asked to write down or draw the thing they most enjoy in life, as well as that of which they are most afraid.

A staff member remembered one such interview when a young couple came in with their child who had neck cancer. When asked her greatest fear, the child's mother drew a little grave with a cross. Rather than address the subject in front of the child, the mother said, "What I'm most afraid of is d-e-a-t-h." She spelled it so her child wouldn't understand.

The staff member went on to say that whether children can spell or not, they always know what is happening to them, but when the parents fear death, the children don't feel free to discuss it. They feel they must shield their parents because their parents couldn't handle it.

She said that when one of the children at the center came out of remission and found out he would probably die, the other children were fascinated and wanted to know what it was like to know he would most likely die, what he was thinking, and how he thought it would be when he was dead. "He told them, I think what happens is, you discard your body, which was never real in the first place, and then you go to heaven to be one soul with all souls. Then, sometimes, you come back to earth as a guardian angel." That was his concept of death. It wasn't a black door with an abyss on the other side, but rather a door of entrance opening onto another way of being. About three weeks before his death, the other children wanted to visit him in the hospital. Having my own hang-ups about it, I worried what they would go through if I took them there. The parents gave them permission to go, however, so we went. At the hospital, I saw the kids were there for only one reason, to give the dying child their love and support. On the way home, I overheard two of them. "You know he's going to die, don't you?" said one. "Yes, I'm so glad we came," answered the other.

Irene Ellis, a gifted school teacher, talked about how she included a student's death in her classroom, and the naturalness with which the child's nine-year-old classmates accepted the process.

"I was aware David was dying from the moment he was brought in for his first-grade interview. At the end of our meeting, his father told me he had leukemia but that everything was under control.

"David was very delicate. Every two weeks he went to the hospital for injections and observation. Through chemotherapy treatments, he lost every hair on his head. But aside from the toll the disease took on his body, I felt there was something beautiful about his whole being: the way he painted, his devotion and eagerness to learn, and a certain charm and sweetness about him that brought something special into the class.

"I felt disturbed by what I sensed was his mother's unwillingness to face up to the fact of David's death. If he became ill, it was always his father who would come to get him.

"At the end of each morning, he would be very tired and I would sometimes lay him down on a soft rug. I would tell the others to keep their voices down and they loved him enough to stay quiet.

"They all knew he was sick and when he was coming to the end of his life, and had been absent from school for many weeks, I told them there might come a time when David would not be back in school.

"Very early in the fourth grade, when he had been in my class exactly three years, he died. At the time, I was teaching the class about the Norse gods, about Odin coming to earth and returning to heaven across the rainbow bridge, and so I spoke about David having gone on his journey over the rainbow bridge.

"On the day of David's funeral, we spent the first part of class singing the songs and repeating the poems David had loved best. I had suggested all the children bring flowers to school and they worked in groups, making the most beautiful floral wreaths and sprays I'd ever seen, which I took to the funeral. They all wanted to go, but it wasn't my place to give them permission.

"After that, the class settled down to conditions without David. For a long time we kept his last painting on the wall, and continued to talk about him whenever his name came up."

Joy Smith, a nurse who set up a hospice (see page 164) in northern California, worked for several years in pediatric oncology.

"In every case, it was the child who renewed my strength in the process of his or her dying. Very rarely were they ever afraid. They were, in fact, gracious and beautiful about saying their good-byes and expressing how much they loved and appreciated their families and the hospital staff.

"There was a sixteen-year-old girl who died at the

hospital. She was at the age where children generally go through a lot of consciousness about their bodies and hers had been completely altered by the chemotherapy. She had gone bald from the treatment. Besides that, she had always been shy. The day before she died, Henry Winkler, the actor, visited the hospital. She wanted to see him very much but couldn't leave her bed to go to the auditorium, so we asked him if he would visit her in her room and he agreed. I thought he would be repulsed by the way she looked but it didn't seem to affect him at all. He was very genuine and friendly with her and they spent a lot of time together. Her parents were there, too, and so was I and we all had a wonderful time, laughing and giggling.

"The next morning, she was very difficult to arouse and when she did awake, it was to say good-bye to us all, to tell us she loved us and that she wasn't afraid."

Judy Conley, a social worker, counsels children who have the life-threatening illness cystic fibrosis, and their parents.

"The kids that have to cope with this disease seem to mature faster than their peers and acquire a wisdom other children of their age lack. It's as if they're experiencing things most people won't experience until they're much older.

"Most of the adolescents I've worked with seem more ready for their deaths than their parents are. The teens are concerned with how their parents are going to feel about it; what will happen to their mothers and fathers after they are dead. I think this concern about their parents hinders the childrens' ability to work through the things they need to work through before they die."

Pat Taylor, a coordinator of the Center for Attitudinal Healing, discussed how she had allowed dying children to make a contribution to her life.

"I used to be very frightened of death and saw it as a great void and as something painful, where I would be alone and set apart from others. What I've learned from these children is that we have spirits, that we are connected, and that love transcends everything. Seeing the courage, bravery, and love of these children has made me realize there may be something more after this life. They handled their deaths so much better than did the adults surrounding them."

Unlike their parents, children do not have to continually pretend that they know everything. They can allow themselves the luxury of not knowing, to simply be open to experience, to let in what is. In the area of death and dying, there is much to be learned from our children.

*BESS:*

When Jack left me, I attempted suicide. Apparently, I got very close to dying. I had gone into my room and closed the door, after taking a large amount of sleeping pills. Because I had dealt with the strife between my husband and me in a very self-pitying way, my two daughters hadn't wanted to see me much, so a whole night and part of a day went by until they came into my room, found me on the floor, and rushed me to the hospital to have my stomach pumped.

I did not want to be brought back and I don't remember going in an ambulance. All I recall is being somewhere with bright lights and saying, "No. No. I don't want to come back." I felt quite separated from my body. However, it was very important for me to come back to deal with what followed.

My youngest daughter, Diane, had been complaining of knee pains for a long time. When she was sixteen, this was diagnosed as being related to a large inoperable cancerous tumor in her pelvis.

I believe she became vulnerable to whatever it is that makes cancer unfold between the time Jack told me he wanted to leave and the time he actually left, and it was related to all the antics I went through in dealing with that. She loved her father very much and she was angry with both him and me. At the same time, her older sister had also left home, partially because of everything going on between Jack and me. Diane missed her very, very much. I think those three things —the loss of her father, her sister, and her good opinion of me contributed to her illness.

Diane and I were together at the pediatrician's when she was first told. It was shocking, totally unbelievable. For a few days, we acted as if she had been told she had measles. But we were too close to pretend with each other for long.

We knew Diane would be hospitalized as little as possible and we would do almost everything on an outpatient basis. At that time, Jack and I came to know that what had to be lived through, we would all live through together. We had absolutely no conflict in that. So he came back home and we all shared it.

We were introduced to a doctor who was experimenting with a process known as the "transfer factor," which involved borrowing some of Jack's white blood cells for Diane. We chose this method of treatment. Whether or not it prolonged Diane's life, I don't know. However, when her tumor was discovered she was given six weeks to live and, in fact, lived two more years.

I shared with a lot of people outside my family. It may be it was easy for me to do this because those people did not know how I was before Diane's diagnosis. Up until then, I was a very dependent person. Leah, my oldest daughter, still saw me in those terms, but those who met me later on knew a very different person. I felt if I could live through this time with grace, then I could live through anything else on earth with grace. I had been an introspective person but I got stronger.

Also, I had also been role-bound. I got married during World War II, when the whole Freudian, iron-cast *gestalt,* which has done so much harm to women, was really flourishing. The typical role for women was one of subservience, and I carried the need to be subservient much further than was necessary. Diane's illness, however, stripped me down to the bone. I no longer had time to play that game anymore, to pretend I was something I wasn't or wasn't something I was.

I feel Diane stayed around until she decided it was time to go. And when she decided, she went. It was like pulling down a blind.

The transfer factor, which seemed to have kept the cancer in her body from metastasizing to her lungs, was also bringing with it a great deal of pain, so she stopped the transfer factor. She had also chosen not to have radiation any more. She feared what it would do to her body and wanted the time left to her to be good time.

I went through times of wishing it were over, thinking we had saved her, wanting to bear the pain for her. I went through times of absolute triumph when we conquered the pain. We went to a very, very fine neurosurgeon who performed a cordotomy to sever the nerves in her spine which were carrying the message of pain, after which Diane was able to give up all her painkillers.

One day in October, our family was entertaining guests, one of whom was a young girl who knew Diane had played the flute. The girl asked if she could borrow the flute and play it and Diane said yes. When the girl played, it seemed to me Diane reexperienced the loss of her own ability to play the instrument. After they left, Diane said she felt very tired. My husband carried her to her bed. He held her and she lay down. I was at the foot of the bed. Then, she looked into my eyes, and what she was seeing, I don't know, but her eyes held a look of surprise and wonderment. You know, I would not give up that experience for anything in my life. And she died.

It was life-altering. Who could be the same?

My first reaction to her death was relief. The next thing I did was to go into her bedroom and take out every evidence of illness and throw it into the garage. I was relieved to have the illness part over. That was the part I buried. The rest of her is part of me and that I'll never lose.

My relationship with Jack is a very different one now. We recognize we are two separate people who are living together because we want to live together, not because we think we have to. We know that as a result of our child's illness, we have shared together more than we could possibly share with anyone else.

I feel eventually we must all relinquish our children. I had to relinquish my oldest daughter and I relinquished her to life. I wish I could have relinquished Diane to life, also. But you give them up anyway.

I have an awareness of the preciousness of the time on earth now that I never had before, and I live my life with the constant awareness that it may end at any time and that each day is very precious, not in terms of what I can get out of it but in terms of what I can put into it.

Jack and I don't talk much about the sorrow. We know we both have it. Leah doesn't talk much about it but we know she has it. It's like a bond the three of us have. We have reminders of Diane all around the house, pictures of her, a portrait done by a friend.

It helps me to have visual reminders and it's also painful. I don't think it's a masochistic experience but a refusal to give up somebody who was tremendously important. And it's worth the pain for the richness of not shutting your life off from that person and continuing the dialogue. She plays a constant part in my life.

Unfortunately, in a culture in which death is denied and comfort is prized above all else, until very recently it was considered desirable to exhibit a stiff upper lip after a death, to be a "tower of strength" to others. The attendant characteristics of suppressing experience, and the cost of maintaining such a pretense, are virtually ignored. Time and again we read that parents don't ever expect to get over feeling sad about the death of a child. There exists the feeling that if we were to get over feeling sad, it would be a betrayal of that child.

Ironically, it seems that clinging to pain is actually an attempt to avoid experiencing the pain of loss.

"Aversion to pain causes a lot of people to seek experiences in which they will be able to keep away the pain. Seeking to get away from pain causes us most of the pain in our lives. When there are life experiences that are unacceptable because they are painful, then you don't have room for reality because reality is sometimes painful. If you spend your life avoiding the little pains, you are completely unprepared for the big ones. In trying to be secure, to be comfortable, to be invulnerable, you make your world smaller and smaller until you are imprisoned in what you consider to be safe. Thus livingness is traded off for an arbitrary safeness," says Stephen Levine.

In 1976, David M. Kaplan headed a research team that looked into the impact of childhood leukemia on families. Forty families were surveyed after the death of a child with leukemia. Only 12 percent emerged from the experience without serious damage to effective family functioning and/or multiple problems among the survivors. Five percent experienced a divorce*; 18 percent a separation;

*The low number of divorces was partially attributed to the fact that the survey was taken within three months of the death. In later contacts, divorces increased significantly.

70 percent serious marital problems; 95 percent reported health problems among the survivors; 35 percent had a member under psychiatric care; 25 percent reported a psychosomatic disorder in one member (such as ulcers, colitis, or hypertension); 40 percent reported drinking as a serious problem.

Forty-three percent reported at least one child with school problems; 60 percent described an adult as having serious work problems; 43 percent reported significant difficulty in the mother's homemaking ability. Eighty-eight percent reported morbid grief reactions in at least one member*.

Dr. Kaplan attributed these problems to the following factors: expectations and an unwillingness to tell the truth.

"In our survey, many people hadn't anticipated the death of the child, when there were a hundred reasons they should have, when there were all kinds of confirmation of the bad news. While some families were able to take in that information and use it to their own benefit, others couldn't and seemed totally surprised when their children died. Nowadays, we don't expect children in our society to get seriously sick or die. In the old days, if you had ten kids and five survived that was great. Everybody now figures children are all going to live and we're not prepared for the possibility of them dying.

"The motto Prepare for the worst and hope for the best

*These reactons included 1) daily visits to the cemetery; 2) 'enshrining' the effects of the deceased, i.e. building special shelves for toys, photos, and other belongings; 3) the absence of any voluntary references to the child during the interview.

is a good idea. If you prepare for the worst, then there are no surprises. In the families where this didn't happen, there were a lot of recriminations. Usually the wife had taken the child to the clinic. She was aware of the truth of what was happening, but when she approached her husband, he would say, 'I don't want to hear the bad news. We're going to keep an optimistic viewpoint.' Such women became very angry. They didn't feel their husbands were there to support them.

"If there is such a trait as the ability to be realistic, to be honest, I would say that is the personality ingredient for successful bereavement work. To be able to know and feel and act as if you are in a bad situation; to live with that, to react to that and to let everyone else in the family do that; and to console each other will leave you with the least amount of problems."

There is ample opportunity, after a child's death, to attempt to evade what there is to go through—to deny; to become trapped in "if only's," as if we could ever really go back and undo what has been done; to blank out, through drink or drugs or unconsciousness, the turmoil of intense emotions.

*JEANNE:*

I had my fourth child, a boy, nearly thirty years ago. This was my second husband's first boy and he was thrilled to have a son. We brought him home from the hospital after three days. The next week the baby became sick. The doctor couldn't figure out what was wrong and he became sicker and weaker, eventually being put into an incubator at the hospital where he died a week later.

I never thought he would die. I kept thinking he'd come through it.

My husband and I tried not to show each other how upset we were. I pushed all my grief down and all my friends talked about what a brick I was, as if that were very commendable.

Whenever I was with people, I hid my sadness. I seemed very much in control, discussing the baby's death with people as if I were giving a weather report. I thought by being strong it would set a good example for the children. Consequently, none of us got to deal with our grief. In retrospect, I think there should have been crying and hollering. We should have all had a chance to express it. I still have residual pain over that child's death and my forty-year-old son continues to have trouble dealing with illness and death.

Joan Sheldon, a grief counselor, has found that the loss of a family member tends to bring up past losses. And in counseling people for one particular death, she often finds herself counseling them for some previous loss as well.

In a child's death, there is a possibility that everything in our lives we've ever deemed a failure will be brought up to add to the current experience; we will be certain we have failed and we are the victim of circumstances. Once this is the case, we may wait for circumstances to improve and thus remove us from our lot.

In order to continue through the grief process, rather than to remain bogged in it, we must actively choose to allow ourselves to think the thoughts we have and to feel the feelings we have: to be sad when we are sad, rather than wish or hope to be happy; to be happy when we are happy, rather than think we should be feeling sad for a certain period of time; to be angry, indifferent, excited, dull, when those responses are appropriate, which is when they are happening within us. In truth, we can either let be what is or attempt to avoid what is.

*LOUISE:*

Two of my children have died, one of sudden infant death syndrome; the other in an accident.

The one who died as a baby was a boy, my fourth child. I love children; but at the time, having four was overwhelming. It was a lot of physical work. My baby cried a lot. And no matter what I did for him, he continued to cry. Many times, I took him to the doctor and asked "Why doesn't he stop? Why isn't he happy when I do all this stuff for him?" The doctor couldn't find anything wrong.

Thanksgiving Day he didn't sleep well, but he hadn't cried much that day either. He was two months old, and my husband and kids had played with him all day. In the afternoon, he began to get fussy. We were going for a ride so we put him in his basket in the back seat of the car, on his stomach, where he usually slept. After the ride, he was asleep. So I carried the basket into the back room and left him, shut the door, came out and fed the other children and started his formula. I heard him crying and thought he'd just have to wait because it wasn't ready. Then he became quiet. About an hour-and-a-half later, I decided to wake him up and feed him. The light in the back room was off, so I felt my way over to him. He felt strange—cold and limp. When I brought him into the kitchen, his face was black. Still, I didn't think he was dead.

I immediately called the doctor. It didn't occur to me to call a rescue unit or the fire department. He told me to give the baby rectal stimulation and said he'd be right over. The baby's bonnet was on, tied with a bow. I cut it off, thinking it was choking him, though it had been actually tied loosely. When the doctor came, he said the child was dead, and had been for some time.

They literally had to pry the baby from my arms. I became hysterical and my husband began slapping me, saying, "Get hold of yourself. Shut up."

This became a coroner's case and the police came to the house. Twenty-five years ago, there was no recognition of sudden infant death syndrome. I was treated as if I had killed my child. Of course, I thought I had, too. His crying had driven me crazy and many, many times I had thought, "I can't stand this. Why don't you just get out of here?"

The doctor testified to the police that the child's lungs had been filled with fluid and he had died of an as-yet-unnamed disease. After the autopsy, the police backed down and dropped charges.

Of course, the accusation remained as I thought I had done it.

The way I handled the death was to overwhelm one of my other children with affection. We became very close. After she and a child born after the death went off to school and I no longer had a little one at home, I had to face the issue of the death again. I even bought a dog and carried him around like a child. Eventually, I became psychotic in order to remove myself from life. Ellen, the child with whom I'd become so close, drew a picture of a giraffe and sent it to me in the hospital. Around that time, I reached a turning point, the psychic phenomena I'd been experiencing diminished, and I began to return to normal reality.

Ellen was the source of my happiness for a long time. As she became a teenager and got rebellious, some of that magic wore off.

When she was seventeen, she went to visit her boyfriend's family in Florida. One morning, en route to the dentist, her boyfriend swerved his car to avoid a squirrel, the steering mechanism locked, and the car flipped over. She was killed. Her boyfriend escaped with minor scratches.

I was in California, working nights. I got the phone call as I was getting to bed in the morning. My husband got up to answer the phone. He returned to the bedroom, opened the curtains, and stared out the window. I asked what was going on and he told me the news.

I felt I had to be strong and support the rest of the family. I did a little bit of crying but very quickly pulled myself together, packed, and made arrangements. I called Florida and gave instructions to have her body cremated. By the time I got there, all that was left of her body was ashes.

I quit my job, moved to Florida, and began walking up and down the beaches, thinking she was still really alive and if I was just in the right place at the right time,

I would find her. I had a psychotic episode in Florida when I realized I was never going to find her. It snapped me back and my husband and I returned to California.

I had become a nurse and began working on an oncology floor of a hospital. I was dreaming a lot about Ellen and I felt she was talking to me in these dreams. I asked my therapist if he thought this was a figment of my imagination and he said he didn't feel qualified to pass judgment on this. He suggested I speak to Elisabeth Kübler-Ross. I wrote to her and she told me she was holding a workshop nearby. When I told her I couldn't come because of the expense, she said to bring my sleeping bag and pay her back some time when I could afford it.

During the workshop, I realized that for me, dreaming and thinking about Ellen was a way of trying to hang on to her, which I did because of the mileage I got out of it with myself and other people. I saw I could spend the rest of my life cashing in on this tragedy. I could always say to myself, "Let's feel bad for Louise today," and stay holed up in the house.

Someone there asked Elisabeth if you could ever be completely free of the pain and grief that accompanies the death of someone you love. She replied, "Only when you're finished with it." I saw I was ready to be complete with Ellen's death. I was able to finally let go of her.

After that, I began to actively work with dying people in my hospital. Other nurses started referring their dying patients to me and I would go to their rooms, stay with them, talk with them if that was appropriate. This work has been a source of great satisfaction in my life.

I have since gone to work with a doctor in private practice in which we use stress reduction, biofeedback, and do counseling in life and death transitions.

# 2

She looked over the side of the bridge. Thousands and thousands of tons of boiling white water poured over the fall.

This is the way her little girl had come and had been thrown downriver along with the torrent. She had been running and now she stopped, staring over the bridge. She turned to a man fishing.

"My baby has just gone over the falls. Just watch me. I don't know what I'm going to do."

She thought she would kill herself. Then she thought of her son and knew she wouldn't, not now, maybe later, when he was more able to take care of himself.

She turned and ran back to her campsite. As she went, she talked to her daughter.

"It doesn't mean we didn't love you or want you. Wherever you are, we love you, we are with you."

Her son asked if she had found his sister.

"No. She's dead."

She and her husband held the boy for a long, long

time. Then, while waiting for the rangers to come, she sat in the car by herself. And the full knowledge struck her. Her daughter was dead. This was the way it was. What had happened happened. There was no way to undo it. It was exactly that way. She was dead.

At the same time, she knew she was choosing to have her life be about living, rather than about death, that she was willing to go through whatever there was to go through, rather than cling to the tragedy of the event.

□

Up until the time of the workshop, she had wanted her son back, in the flesh. Nothing else would do. Life was not good enough without him. In the workshop, after she had let herself feel everything she needed to feel; think all the thoughts she had been keeping down; said exactly what she needed to say about it, all that was left was here and now, the present. She knew he wasn't coming back. Finally, it was okay.

□

She thought about her teenage daughter while unfolding the afternoon paper. Jeanie wasn't home yet and hadn't called. On the front page was a picture of a red sports car. It was in color, crushed like an accordion. She turned to her husband.

"Jeanie's dead."

Everyone said no.

"There are other red sports cars. She'll be home. Don't worry."

In that moment, she knew her daughter was dead and, at the same time, she felt as if a weight had come off of her shoulders, as if she'd just finished a big job. She felt calm and peaceful.

At last she called the police and confirmed what she already knew. She cried and cried. She felt there were two of her, the one who was crying and the one who stood calmly by, watching the whole event. On the one hand, it was a catastrophe. On the other, she experienced it as being perfect.

□

People who move through the grief process more quickly than others (within a year of their child's death) begin in this way: they accept the truth of the situation, and they opt for life. They choose not to have their lives revolve around their child's death, but to include that death as a part of their lives. It is also notable that these people are engaged in some sort of spiritual path, not one that we would necessarily associate with organized religion, but some conscious observaton of the forces of the world or universe and their relationship to it.

For them, their lives move on from the event of the death and do not orbit around it. It is not that they no longer cry or sometimes feel angry or frustrated or hopeless or that they don't care their children are dead. There is not one of them who, if given the choice, would not choose to have their child back, but their lives are no longer revolving around that death. And from that, they allow the death of their child to enhance and contribute to the quality of their lives. They use the lessons learned to make them more able and useful to others. While they are not embittered, they are sad sometimes. And while the death is not shut off or forgotten, it is integrated into their lives.

What is accepting things as they are really like? It means if we are thinking about our child, then we think about him, rather than resist or suppress the thought. If we are not thinking about him, then we don't. If we are crying, we cry. And if we are laughing, we laugh. If we feel sad, we feel sad. And if happy, we feel happy. Accepting things as they are is a very natural process, though not a very normal one except, perhaps, to children. Most of us have grown up wanting to be happy when we are sad, or wanting to sit when we are standing.

Accepting things as they are and opting for life is a matter of choice. We can accept life the way it is or we can attempt to have it the way it isn't, to live in the past or to try to make it different. We can be the author of our lives or can be controlled by our circumstances. If one is willing and courageous enough to experience life, the death of his child becomes a contribution and life can be lived as a tribute to that child, as if that child's life had made a difference.

For many people, after a child's death, the initial shock will blanket pain. Numbness will prevail. Eventually, the pain will cut through, waking us to the fact that our child is dead. At this point, one chooses to either embrace the pain and allow it to pass through us, or knock it into submission for a while. Pain can be regarded as a friend or an enemy. By putting it in the position of an enemy, we create a formidable opponent, one we must continually ignore or fight, one for which we will need great vigilance. However, if we allow the pain to be, we can allow it to pass through us and out of us.

Pain is a signal. Just as a toothache wakes us up to the fact there is work to be done on our teeth, so the pain of the death of a child wakes us up to the fact of that death and that there is work to be done on ourselves.

The following is an interview with a man whose eleven-year-old daughter was murdered.* She had gone out to play tennis with a girlfriend and they were both found later, dead. What followed for him was the need to answer those questions that arose as a result of the death of his beloved child: What is the meaning of death and why do I fear it?

It was a tremendous shock, ungraspable, beyond the scope of the boundaries I'd set up for my existence. I didn't have any framework for it. But I wasn't numb. I did a lot of expressing—crying, screaming, whatever.

I used Sarah's killer for my anger and expressed that anger for months. At the trial, there wasn't a thing I could do about my rage except look at him again and again. I began to see things in myself that I didn't know existed. *I* had enough anger to actually kill someone. Every night I would chop wood and I'd fantasize about who I was chopping. Though I've recognized greater compassion for others as a result of Sarah's death, I haven't felt compassion for her killer.

In the beginning, my wife and I spent a lot of time together, but as things subsided, and we began to touch ground a little more, we needed to have our own space to explore, process, and integrate this thing.

I had to work out what had happened to Sarah and what it meant. I trusted no one and nothing except what I could feel and know inside about what was true. I *had* to have the truth.

*In 1979, 6,048 people under the age of twenty-four were murdered in the United States.

I was extremely rigorous with myself about it and my process was very, very painful and took a long time. I experienced the pain of loss and the helpless, hopeless reaching out, of wanting my child and not being able to have her. That led me along, step by excruciating step. I knew I wouldn't quit until I had the truth about death.

At some point, I recognized that my rational mind, highly skilled and developed as it is, is not the whole of who I am. I saw I couldn't depend upon it for the understanding I was seeking. The issue for me was one of faith and doubt. I had to allow faith to develop in me and doubt to flow through me. At one point, my family and I visited a spiritual teacher, Ram Dass, who confirmed for me some of my own conclusions.

Though in the beginning I felt a tremendous loss, my experience of Sarah altered into one of feeling she and I were one being. She was in my heart and I in hers. That comes and goes. When it's present, I feel complete. When it's not, I notice a physical longing for her.

I've learned not to fight my emotions, but to allow them to be. Something like, "Ah, here comes anger. Here comes terrific pain. Here comes loss. Here comes sadness." When I just allow those emotions to be, they turn into incredible grace. From that, I noticed I could allow my thoughts to be as well. That I can just let them be.

Painful as it is, I feel Sarah's death was also meant to be. Just as each moment is meant to be. Though I don't understand it, and have little control over life's processes, if any, I can choose to learn from them or not.

In accepting the death of a child, our processes and the way we manifest them, will differ according to our personalities, our temperaments, our backgrounds, our cultures, and other variables.

In western society, men are expected to be "strong" and "hold things together." Constrained by our cultural agreements, not only do many men hold themselves in contempt when they express tenderness and sorrow, but other men and women may see such expressions as shocking. Often, such mechanisms operate on a level so unconscious, they are unrecognizable even to people trying to transcend them.

Marty Enriquez, a social worker and founder of a support group for parents who have experienced a neonatal death, said that while she sympathized with the fact that fathers are often left out of the grieving process, she was surprised when she noticed how uncomfortable she felt in the presence of a father who was sorrowing openly.

"His wife was the one who was comforting him. He couldn't function at work because he was crying all the time. I hadn't seen that before and was quite amazed by it."

Conversely, one man said of his own grief process, "I was crying and, at the same time, I was relieved I was able to cry because, before that, even though my insides were churning, I was trying to keep everything very matter of fact.

Despite these examples, most fathers will express publicly only those emotions they feel are acceptable for men to display, for example, anger.

The following is one father's experience of the death of his son, followed by excerpts from the father's diary.

The five of us were in the car: my wife; my daughter, less than a year old; my oldest daughter, 5; my son Cody, almost 4; and I. Angela was driving, and as we came off the freeway, she lost control of the van. It went off a little cliff and flipped over once. Everyone was thrown around, but there wasn't a scratch on anyone except Cody, who had hit his head. Though he wasn't visibly bleeding, he was unconscious.

An ambulance arrived and took us to the hospital. Everyone but Cody was put into one room. He was taken to a room where intensive work was done on patients. When we had been in our room forty-five minutes, a doctor came in and said, "I'm sorry. Your son is dead."

After that, it's hard to remember the chain of events. We went into the other room and huddled around Cody. I said the Hebrew prayer, the *Sh'ma.* Then I called some friends. I felt numb and disoriented.

The hospital people didn't seem able to relate to us on an emotional level. For instance, after the doctor had made his original announcement of Cody's death, he sat down, ignoring us, and began filling out forms. None of the staff seemed trained to handle a situation like ours.

I went through the funeral in a fog. My brother made the arrangements and I simply let everything happen. As long as there were people to help me, I let them handle things because I didn't feel I was the right person to do it.

Cody's death was the greatest shock I'd ever experienced. Though I'd been through my father's death, it was different. I had been living far away from him and hadn't been around to see his day-by-day deterioration. When I'd gotten the news of his death, I felt fairly detached. After all, I had my own family. And though I felt a loss and wished we could have shared more years together, I had somehow expected that death, while Cody's was sudden. And Cody was my child.

For a long time, I went through "if onlie's." I avoided the section of freeway where the accident had occured, even if I had to drive long distances out of my way to do that.

I had dreams of Cody. In one, I was downstairs and he was at the top of the stairs. He was being carried off by a group of football players. He seemed fine, happy. There he was, waving good-bye, going off to play.

Six months after the accident, I was selling books at a conference on death and dying. While there, I attended a seminar on psychodrama where I volunteered to reinact the accident. A group of people played the parts of my family, while one hundred others stood around us in a circle. The session was incredibly cathartic for me. Everyone around was crying.

The death made me more sensitive and appreciative of my other children. I began to see how fragile the whole set-up of life is. Also, I lost a lot of my fear of dying. I had an image of walking through the gates of death with my father holding one of my hands, and Cody the other.

*October 4, 1973*

(Two weeks after the death)

My state of mind has altered since Cody's death. It is clear to me that the event has allowed something to occur in me that nothing else in the world could have allowed. I have been thrown into what I can only describe as a "psychedelic" state of mind. In such a state, with its deepened sensibilities, internal emotional triggers, detachment from ordinary life and disorientation, realities are floating about me. I now have on one side a wife and two children and on the other side, Cody. My hands are outstretched to them all. They are equally real, equally loved, equally objects of my sense of responsibility. But how does one fulfill responsibility to a dead four-year-old son? The second day after his death, I fell into a light slumber. I felt a great peace and felt that Cody was there. I felt for a moment I wanted to stay with him and forget this side entirely.

*October 6, 1973*

I am a distracted man and much changed in two weeks. I realized how Cody is a great bond between Angela and myself—internal and invisible. She has said she will be there to help me and to be a stable element, and I will need it. I need to share this sorrow and loss. She is the only one who can do this. In the outside world, there is only misunderstanding, fear, and guilt as I walk through the streets. Our strangeness is grown and I feel it difficult to operate on the street. It is painful to confront people who don't know of Cody's change of state.

In some ways, Cody's death means only this to me: to become as fully human as possible. Will this resolve last? The feelings otherwise are very desperate and hard to bear.

*November 11, 1973*

(Five weeks later)

I am crying. This morning, I awoke with the memory of Cody's voice. The voice struck me as beautiful and perfect and I am filled with a longing that is breaking my heart. I went into his room and opened his drawers one by one. The familiar clothes—his pajamas, his pants and shirts, evoke him so really for me that my longing for him is intense. And longing can only get more intense or, to some extent, be forgotten. It can only be ended by achieving the object of longing. On our bodily level, that cannot be satisfied.

*December 14, 1973*

(Two months later)

I am going to try to go to San Francisco. We'll see. I feel good tonight. Perhaps because of the season of the year. Perhaps because business is good. But I remember my son, and I miss him. It is a reminder of the transience of all this. Still, there are so many things to work out. It is in the form of my relationship with Angela. Some of it is good, but so much can get between us. I accuse her of being thin-skinned with me. And yet, it is I who am so with her. The answer: live, accept, love, trust, and always try to grow. What choice do I have? Grow or die. Just as I must let Cody go his way, so there is no choice considering Angela or anyone else.

*December 24, 1973*

(Two-and-a-half months later)

Lately, I have reacted to the swift passage of time as a good thing. The swifter, the better. I find it difficult to organize my thoughts. The only thing I can keep my thoughts on is my *t'ai chi* practice: keeping my body relaxed and the *t'ai chi* flowing. Cannot think too well this morning.

*January 1, 1974*

(Three months later)

Back to Philadelphia after a visit to New York City and my family. Visiting my brother's house, I was haunted by my son. Cannot write . . . cannot think . . .

*February 23, 1974*

(Four-and-a-half months later)

In my dream, we all sat down to play a game. I am told the game is played with two-sided pieces. I am to start at Go, which is somewhere in the middle. By means of the pieces, I will supposedly work out my life. It sounds simple. Then I am told to use only the back of the piece and to play without knowing the markings. I am being monitored by a line of scientific-looking men. I cannot move my pieces and stop playing. A little boy begins playing the game. He does it easily and simply, making the correct moves. He turns to the scientist/monitors and begins to chastise them, telling them they have been harsh and unkind to me; that I have a good heart and can do better. As I awoke, I remembered what was the one force that prevented me from moving, the thing that prevented me and this little boy from being together. It was death.

*September 11, 1974*

(Eleven months later)

I understand. I don't understand. It's different now. Yes, time does change it all. I start right now. I stand in the present and face the future. Our love is growing, our spirit is growing, our happiness is growing. Every day is not just a trip through space but an opportunity, renewed to be and to grow in our being. What had to be was. What will be will be. There is no loss without gaining, no parting without rejoining, no death without birth. We have refrained from wishing him back with us as much as possible, for his growth requires that. After all, we could only call him back into his past. We cannot hold things we love by force or desire. If we let them go, they return in the form and in the time/space frame that is best for their own self-expression.

# 3

Our culture includes very little open, honest communication about death. Rather than to bring it into the light, we seek to suppress and mask our thoughts and feelings about it. We would rather our conversations remained "pleasant" and that we remained "comfortable." John Golenski, chaplain of Oakland Children's Hospital, says, "When a middle class white child dies, there are four people at the hospital at the most. But if a hispanic or black child dies, I can expect to see twenty or thirty people." Albert Knittel, for many years a funeral director in San Francisco, says, "We still see full funerals and ritualized grieving periods in certain ethnic groups. For example, Filipinos, Samoans and Latinos express themselves openly at the death of their children. However, the whites who come here tend to hold their grief down and show very little emotion."

As mentioned before, one study showed that 75 percent of the parents who have lost a child have serious marital problems within a year of the death. This statistic is symptomatic of an inability to communicate.

Often, husbands and wives will experience the death of their child in different ways. Not only may their experiences be different, but the manner in which they grieve will also be different. It is not the differences that create marital problems; it is a lack of communication about these differences and a willingness for each parent to recognize and sanction these differences so they can mutually exist without causing a rift.

John Golenski says, "Despite variables, I think women and men react differently to the loss of a child. For a woman, the child is not only a loved object and a person in whom the future is invested, but a woman losing a child in our culture is also a failure in the primary definition of what it means to be a woman, namely a mother. And she's been mutilated in the sense that a part of her that has come out of her body has been destroyed.

"The loss of a child, for a mother, is the most difficult thing to undergo in life. Perhaps, more difficult than having a terminal illness herself. It is different for most males. Men, particularly white, middle-class men, are not allowed to express their feelings. They are supposed to be in charge, in control. You hear men use that term a lot. I once counseled a father whose fear of 'losing control' was so great, he excused himself to go to the bathroom every time he thought he would cry during our conversation, so that he could 'gain control' again."

While women are angered by what they feel is a lack of sensitivity and caring on the parts of their husbands, men express confusion by what they consider to be a too lengthy grieving period on the part of their wives.

In her book *Living with Death and Dying,* Elisabeth

Kübler-Ross noted that while many times mothers stayed home in a state of shock and denial, fathers went to work, spending time with other people and being occupied with other matters, thus proceeding to the stage of anger more quickly than their wives.

After the death of a child, parents need the opportunity to sort it out for themselves. A coordinator and grief counselor of the Shanti Project says, "I would strongly suggest that people let go of their agendas after the death of someone they love."

We need to give ourselves permission to have our own experience, despite what other people think and, especially, despite what we fear other people will think.

It is not necessary for parents to experience the death of a child in the same way. Most probably they won't. What is important is for each family member to allow the other their own experience no matter how different; and to respect the other's experience.

Of equal importance is that parents communicate with each other, to allow each other into their lives—their thoughts, feelings, judgments—and to create an environment of safety, where no one need bury his experience for fear it will be unacceptable.

Crucial to the building of a safe environment is the manner in which things are communicated. If we believe that the other person is to blame for the way we feel, communication freezes. If we know that we are responsible for the way we feel and communicate in a way that expresses that, there is a good chance of establishing a territory in which anything can be said, anything can be expressed.

The fastest way to block communication is to take the position that it is the other person's fault that we are in a bad way. For example, "I was angry because he didn't show emotion"; "I was irritated because she wouldn't stop being sad."

When a child dies we are likely to experience turbulent emotions, emotions many of us are not skilled in working with, emotions we may be more used to suppressing than experiencing. The temptation is to bury them again and live in pretense, or to use them as weapons, hurling them at each other, engaging rather in battle than the painful job of living without a child.

So it isn't the differences in experiences that create alienation between partners, it is the unwillingness to communicate about how it is for each of us, and to communicate in a way that is open and honest, that actually intends to have the other person know our experience.

Very often, the cost of closing down communication is the end of the relationship.

"After my daughter's death, I began to feel I had put too much of my life into my family and that was now dangerous for me. Staking so much on other people meant my stability depended on them—on whether my husband and our other child stayed alive. I knew I had to change my lifestyle. I didn't want to be my husband's wife anymore. Because he still wanted to have the kind of marriage where I stayed home most of the time, eventually our relationship blew up and we separated."

Even for spouses who are normally communicative, the death of a child often produces an atmosphere of isolation, of separateness. Although in our cultural mythology, death is a time that draws people together, this is generally not so. Individuals who are unused to and unskilled at sharing themselves with others will not suddenly, miraculously extend themselves.

*ARLENE:*

I felt something was wrong during my pregnancy with David, though I couldn't articulate it. I didn't talk about it to anyone either because I was superstitious and felt if I put it into words then something really would go wrong. I had never had those feelings about my pregnancy with my first child.

David's birth was unusual. My labor needed to be induced after my water broke and I didn't have contractions. When he was born, I was delirious and angry with everybody. Randy stayed with me every step of the way.

When David was nine months old he got an ear infection. I took him to the doctor for a routine checkup and the doctor palpated his stomach and found a lump. He said he hoped it wasn't a tumor. He sent us to a hospital for X-rays.

The day was a nightmare. I was working as a psychiatric social worker and had patients scheduled for that day, but when I left work for the doctor's I would not come back for five months.

David was given a kidney function test and the results showed there was an abnormality. One kidney was almost destroyed.

I went through the day seemingly in control but when I reached home, I got as far as the garage and started crying and crying. The doctor had said there was a good chance it was cancer. I was incredibly stunned and shocked. I felt disoriented, terrified, and didn't know what to do. I just kept looking at my baby. I didn't want to let him go into that hospital.

He was found to have a very fast-growing malignancy called a Wilm's Tumor. We checked him into a hospital with a parent care program in which parents were allowed to sleep next to their child, administer all medication, and help in the child's care. There was also a supervised playroom for siblings.

David had a battery of horrible, horrible tests. Randy and I alternated staying with him. Randy was there when David had a bone marrow test, which is very painful, done in the leg. Randy broke down and started crying. The nursing staff and doctors didn't seem to know how to handle Randy's grief. They all left him alone. On the other hand, the mothers there were always ready to put an arm around me when I needed it. Randy felt very alone.

David was scheduled for surgery when his blood pressure went up into the stroke range. Our urologist had contacted a top pediatrician to do the surgery.

I was waiting near the operating room, when the anesthesiologist came flying through the door, saying,

"Come on. Let's get on with it. My Sunday's been interrupted."

The nurses explained they were waiting for the doctors and for David's stomach to empty. The anesthesiologist said,

"Oh, he's only a kid. His stomach emptied in a couple of hours."

I was absolutely shocked by his attitude. The nurses looked embarrassed. Then he said,

"Where's the mother?"

I said, "Here."

He just gasped. Normally, I would have told someone like that off, but I felt too out of it.

The surgery took around five hours. The hardest part was remembering the look David gave us when he was picked up and taken to the operating room. He looked at us as if he had been betrayed.

He needed radiation and chemotherapy. I was in his room two days after the surgery when he stopped breathing. When I told the nurse she ran around the bed so fast I was knocked against the wall. In a minute, a whole team of people were in the room and one of the other mothers grabbed me aside and held me in her arms while he was put on a respirator and began breathing on his own again.

*RANDY:*

I was very optimistic. I felt everything would be fine. I was looking forward to two years into the future when his survival chances would have greatly increased. I visited David every day after work but mainly I took care of our daughter.

*ARLENE:*

I was allowed to be with him in the intensive care nursery. I met the new nurses at the beginning of every shift. David couldn't seem to understand why I didn't pick him up. I was allowed to stick my head under the tent and press my body against his, which seemed to help.

After he was discharged from the hospital, we

would bring him back for radiation treatments. They would take him into a big room and close the metal door. I could hear him crying through the intercom.

The people at the hospital remarked he appeared to be the most depressed baby they'd ever seen. After surgery, he was frightened of people who wore white, and of all females except his sister and me.

Paula, my daughter, four, couldn't understand what was going on. She thought David was sick because of something she'd done.

One day when I went to the hospital, I saw a little boy who had lymphoma. He had the look of death about him. I saw that in David, too. I was never optimistic about his chances. At one point, the doctor started feeling optimistic and I thought, "Maybe there's something wrong with me." But David kept losing weight, and getting smaller and smaller.

I couldn't get him up one morning. He would wake up and then fall off to sleep. I thought, "He's going to die right here with me and I can't take it."

I took him to the pediatrician's office. He called the hospital and said, "We should hospitalize David to make Arlene feel better." I felt I was being described as a hysterical mother.

Randy and I had started fighting a lot. He didn't want David brought to the hospital and thought he'd do better at home. One day I stayed with Paula and Randy went to the hospital and when I got there, I noticed David's stomach was incredibly large. I yelled at Randy, "What's wrong with him?" He said, "What do you mean?" I said, "You didn't notice?"

*RANDY:*

David died at eleven months and seven days. The day before, he had a respiratory arrest and several cardiac arrests. As I reached the intensive care nursery, I noticed David wasn't breathing. The nurses put him on a respirator and said, "It's going to be all right. Don't worry." The pediatrician came in and told the staff, "If you can keep him going for two days, I'll buy you a case of scotch. Two days are all we need."

I was watching David through a window a little after midnight and the chief resident came out and told me David was dead. I felt like hitting her. Then I started crying. Arlene saw me crying and said, "He's dead. Isn't he?" I said yes and Arlene's mother fainted.

*ARLENE:*

She collapsed on me and I was saying, "My baby." Everybody was crushing me in their rush to comfort me and everyone was crying. Five minutes later, a nurse came up to me and said, "Where would you like the body sent?" I said, "I don't consider that a body, that's still my baby and I want to see him."

I kissed him and held his hand. He didn't look anything like he had alive. His skin had turned dark and was swollen.

When the doctor came upstairs, he didn't know what to say, even after all his experience with families. Finally, he said, "You know, you can still have another baby." I wanted to punch him out.

*RANDY:*

David was cremated. Arlene was medicated and appeared to be very much in control. I wasn't. There's a song I always sing and I requested it be sung at the funeral. I just cried and cried. At the cemetery, I was calm until they put the casket into the ground and started covering it. Then I started crying again. People kept coming up, hugging me, saying they'd always be there.

*ARLENE:*

My father was with us every step of the way. When we went to the funeral parlor before the service, I brought a hat to cover the stitches on David's head. No one was in front of the building so we went in through the back. We looked in through a door and saw David lying on a slab. The funeral director appeared and said, "Oh, my gosh, you weren't supposed to come in this way." He put the hat on David's head and asked me how I liked it. I said it looked fine. Then I said, "You got his color back. But his mouth isn't the way it was." I touched his fingers.

I went through the funeral in a fog. Everything was black and I wanted to wear black, also. Friends said, "People don't wear black to funerals any more." I couldn't believe anyone would try to tell me what to wear to my child's funeral. I felt if I wanted to go naked it was my prerogative to do so.

*RANDY:*

Arlene's parents didn't want us to talk about David's death. Two months later, Arlene's sister had a baby and her parents would bring the baby around, not knowing how much we hated being around it.

*ARLENE:*

My mother said I didn't know what real sadness was, because she had two things to be sad about: the loss of her grandchild and her concern about her daughter. Then she would point out how well she was holding it together as a model for me.

*RANDY:*

For a long time, things were tense between Arlene and I. Then we slowly began talking about how we felt. But at the beginning, we just couldn't hear each other.

When we lose a child, many of us believe because *we* are suffering, because *we* are in pain, it is up to others to communicate with us, to extend themselves to us. Unfortunately, this is not the case. Most of us are pretty much in the same boat regarding our ability to deal with death openly and supportively. The job of initiating communication, which can be looked at as a great opportunity or another burden, is not up to our spouses, our friends, our parents, our co-workers; the job is up to us. It begins with the willingness to accept that life is the way it is, that This Is It, that nobody did it to us, and then to tell the truth about how it is for us—rather than looking for someone to pin it on.

A structure for promoting communication between spouses is a family meeting. Ground rules should include:

- Being open-ended so that each person will be sure to get as much time as he or she needs to say whatever they have to say.
- The intention and willingness to listen and hear each other; the intention to establish a context of support and safety in the family.
- Each person communicates everything until they are complete. While one person is taking his or her turn,

the other simply listens, without the opportunity to refute or rebut what is being said, without reacting and thus cutting off communication.

• Each person tells the other what they want in the way of support.

• Phones are taken off the hook and doorbells unanswered during the meeting.

In a supportive atmosphere, it is all right with him if she is sad. It is fine with her if he is angry. It is acceptable if she grieves at home and he goes off and works. Each one's mode of grieving becomes unique and sacred, rather than divisive.

In moving through the death of a child, there should also be room to express anger, frustration, and sorrow. However, there must be a distinction drawn between expressing it, one to another, and dumping it on each other. For some people, it is appropriate to scream and cry at one another, for others it is not. The most basic rule to follow, perhaps, is that we need to let each other know that while we are acting out our emotions, we are not blaming each other for causing them.

Kübler-Ross's workshop participants beat inanimate objects with rubber hoses; other people punch pillows. The manner in which we express anger is not important. It is imperative, though, to express it.

The jumbled web of our emotions often serves as a barricade, cutting us off from the lessons death has to offer. We tend to become enmeshed in sorrow and anger and are distracted from the reality that exists beyond the chaos—the screen upon which the drama is played out.

Within the experience of a child's death is the opportunity to see love where one was not aware love existed before; to realize that what is really important in life—what is really wanted—cannot pass through the eye of a needle; the chance to transform a relationship.

*MEGAN:*

Thomas was our first child. I was a nurse, and had this feeling that nurses make good mothers. Nothing could go wrong. I would be a good parent.

He weighed nine pounds, three ounces and was the biggest, healthiest, most beautiful child I'd ever seen. I breast-fed and took good care of him. I also handed in my resignation as a public health nurse because I saw that my real commitment was to motherhood.

A strange thing happened after the birth. I told our family and friends about the birth verbally but I didn't sent out birth announcements. Later, I thought of this as being providential.

When Thomas was three months old, he began looking funny—pale—and was less active then he'd been. He also began to vomit. One morning, while nursing, he threw up his hands as if he were choking. After that, every time he nursed, the same thing happened.

Turning him over one morning, I noticed his eyes shifted to one direction. He had a passing seizure. I called the doctor but couldn't get an appointment until late afternoon. By three o'clock, I was going crazy so I picked him up and took him to the doctor. The doctor looked him over, then quietly left the room and came back with a second doctor. They said they would need to have a spinal tap done.

The next few days in the hospital were a nightmare of doctors questioning me all the time. After he began to get antibiotics intravenously, my husband and I thought he would be all right.

That was Friday. Tuesday, while I was holding him, I noticed he was staring and I thought, "He's blind." A neurosurgeon and eye doctor examined him and thought it might be encephalitis. He began to look very bad, as if he were dying. They performed surgery and removed a lot of fluid. We had to start tube-feeding him.

I would go to the hospital every morning at six-thirty and stay until eleven at night. I felt as if I were a failure. I was embarrassed and I was furious. I was sure the nurses weren't taking good care of him. One day they threw his pacifier down the laundry chute. I wouldn't express my anger to any of the nurses except one with whom I was friendly. She made sure a pacifier was pinned to Thomas's clothing after that. I was also feeling very, very sad; and, in trying to save my milk for Thomas, my breasts were always throbbing painfully.

The hospital decided they couldn't treat him because they didn't know what was wrong. Since I was a nurse and could do the same things as the hospital personnel, we took him home where I suctioned him of mucus every fifteen minutes and tube-fed him every few hours.

In the evenings while I slept, my husband took care

of him. Then I watched him for the rest of the time. My friend the nurse was beautiful. She came to the house frequently, once spending the night, so Peter and I could sleep. My mother was also very nurturing, and took care of the house, as well as the rest of us.

When the doctors began to think Thomas had a rare hereditary disease we took him to the medical center. This was a real blow, because if it were true we couldn't have more children. After a week, those doctors came up empty-handed. They said the only way we would know what was wrong was if he died and was autopsied.

My worst fear was that Thomas would need to be institutionalized, as my doctor suggested. He had said Thomas would require constant care and we wouldn't be able to go on with our lives. I wanted my child and I realized what my doctor said was true. We began proceedings to admit him to an institution. Our doctor suggested that we not spend too much time with him and detach ourselves, but Peter and I continued to visit him.

The day before he died, I went to see him and he smiled. The next day, while he was feeding, he aspirated and died. My feelings were very mixed—loss and grief and relief that he wouldn't have to go to an institution.

I thought if only I knew from the beginning he would only live a short while, I would have held him more. I remembered when he was healthy I would give him his pacifier and pat him on the back when he was crying instead of picking him up. If I'd known, all those petty things like feeding him at the proper times wouldn't have mattered.

The autopsy found he had had a brain tumor. I felt, "Okay, we'll have more children."

While my husband had prayed that Thomas would get well, I had prayed that no matter what happened we would be able to handle it.

Peter and I took off. We went to Oregon and bummed around for a week. We left our house. Even though it was brand new with drapes, couch, every kind of new furniture, it meant nothing to us. That week was the best our relationship had ever been. We were totally immersed in one another. Our lives had just gone down to the core and become very simple.

When we returned the loneliness and grief set in. I had nothing to do with myself during the day. I was already pregnant again but didn't know it.

Twice a week, I began working with a sixteen-year-old girl who had cancer. She knew she was dying and I knew she was dying and she knew I knew. We became very close and I was able to talk with her about her death, something I couldn't do with Thomas. She told me she had looked forward to being sixteen but wasn't at all looking forward to seventeen. She said, "I can't even imagine having another birthday." She died a month before her seventeenth birthday.

After Thomas's death, a lot of our so-called friends dropped away. One woman I'd become friendly with when we took natural childbirth classes together would never come around with her own child when Thomas was sick. I hated the fact that her kid made it and mine didn't.

Another woman used to visit me when I was with Thomas in the hospital, bring fruit and say things like, "Boy, I'm so glad nothing's ever happened to my child. I've been so lucky." Once I told her, "You know, your life isn't over yet."

A former patient of mine had left her child with her husband. When Thomas was dying, she called to tell me about this and said she was having a great time, going from place to place with a group of people. I told her, "I don't understand it. Here I am, a good mother. I wanted my child so badly and he's in the hospital dying, while you—who have a perfectly healthy child —left him and are flying around the country. It makes me so angry I can't even talk to you anymore." She probably thought I was crazy. But I couldn't come to grips with my resentment over her behavior and unleashed it.

Two of the nurses I'd worked with completely avoided me; no note, no call, nothing. At first I thought this was their way of telling me they never really liked me but later realized they probably just didn't know what to say.

There was one public health nurse who was extremely supportive. Her own child had died of hyaline membrane disease and when Thomas was dying, she couldn't do enough to help. She came to my house and vacuumed, did laundry, sewed buttons on shirts. She wanted so much to give. It was as if she had been supported through her child's death and she wanted to pass that on to me.

Peter and I were invited to join the local chapter of Candlelighters, an organization for parents of children who have or have had cancer, and within a year, Peter was elected its president. I became a speaker for this group and talked to parents who had lost children, and to a nursing school. I had learned so much from my experience with my son and felt I had to let other people know about them.

I felt Thomas came here to help me grow and teach me something. If he had lived eighty-five years, I couldn't have grown more or loved more than I did in the few months I knew him.

His death took a lot of my values and turned them inside out. I have been humbled by the experience. I know that nothing matters except the quality of life.

Things really turned around after my daughter was born, nine months after Thomas's death. It was bliss. I just let myself spend time with her, feeding her when she wanted to be fed, not worrying about rashes or whether she was getting the proper amount of milk or if I was doing all the right things. Six months after that birth, I became pregnant with my second son. At the time I felt I could never have enough children.

I have since returned to school, in a nurse-practitioner's program.

# 4

Often, in focusing attention on their own needs after the death of a child, parents become insensitive and inaccessible to their other children. Another factor in parental unwillingness to deal honestly with surviving children is that death ranks alongside sex and money as topics we are uncomfortable with and thus consider to be "inappropriate" subjects to discuss with our children.

Children often experience resentment and guilt over the feeling they have been shunted aside during a sibling's terminal illness and/or death. When a parent's discomfort limits his willingness to discuss the death of a child with that child's sibling, the child will draw his own conclusions about the meaning of death and the circumstances of this particular death, ideas that may be highly inaccurate. For example, a child who has been told that a sister or brother has passed away may be certain they will return. They may think the other child has died because they were bad or has died because of something the surviving sibling said or thought about them. Dr. David Kaplan, after interviewing many children whose siblings had died, says, "Another example of recriminations occurs in families where the siblings weren't dealt with honestly. Later, they reproach their parents and ask, 'Why didn't you tell me? I might have behaved differently. If I was being selfish, if I was being jealous, I might have understood a little better.' "

When a child is dying, parents often forget about interacting with the rest of the family. "They forget what the long-term effects are after the child is gone," said a social worker dealing with children who have cystic fibrosis, and their parents. "I've known parents who become so focused on the children with CF, it's obsessive. Nothing else matters. When this happens, the rest of the family is disturbed for many years because the other siblings have been virtually ignored."

Frequently, consciously or unconsciously, parents withdraw from their remaining children because they painfully remind them of the dead child.

*JESSIE:*

Beth was a breach birth. She came six weeks early. During labor, her head got stuck and she was without oxygen for ten minutes. Also, a nerve in her right arm was torn and that caused paralysis. The doctors said she probably wouldn't live and, if she did, her right arm would be paralyzed forever and she would have 50 percent chance of being retarded. By the time she was three months old, her arm was fine and she was bright and alert.

Although she was progressing well, I had a feeling from the beginning that Beth wouldn't live very long. I couldn't imagine her growing up to be an adult and sometimes would find myself thinking about how things would be after she died.

At two and a half, Beth was taken to the doctor for a physical examination, smallpox vaccination, and DPT shot. After a week, Beth complained about a pain in her neck. The doctor saw her and said it was probably a sore throat. When I insisted Beth was complaining about her neck and not her throat, the doctor suggested she didn't know the difference. *I* knew Beth could tell the difference. He told me I was a worry wart, prescribed sore throat medicine, and sent us home.

Beth began sleeping a lot, which wasn't normal for her. The doctor said sleeping a lot was usual for a child with a cold. But she didn't have a cold and continued to get worse, until she was getting dizzy just standing up.

I had my husband, Jim, take Beth back to the doctor because I thought his word would have more force with the doctor. The doctor reluctantly sent them both to the hospital so Beth could be tested for meningitis. We went to one hospital that didn't give that test and had to go to a second where we sat in a waiting room behind twenty other people. Beth began passing out in her seat and when Jim told the receptionist she said we would still have to wait our turn. At this point, Jim said she needed to be tested for polio, which got her scooted into a room immediately. They gave her a spinal tap and screwed it up so that she needed another one. They asked us to allow her to stay in the hospital overnight so she could be tested again in the morning. I stayed in her room until we were asked to leave. She had become suddenly very alert and awake, talking to me, looking out at the city lights and saying how pretty they looked.

The doctor suggested we go home and sleep. He said everything would be fine. When I got home, I was so exhausted I collapsed immediately.

In the morning, I was awakened by Jim yelling at me. He said Beth had gone into a coma and that her heart had stopped. My mind just exploded.

When we reached the hospital with my mother-in-law, we were told they had done brain wave tests and that our daughter was legally dead and we would have to give them permission to turn off the life support systems.

I went into the intensive care unit; she was still lying there, hooked up to tubes. I tried to see if she was still alive. My mother-in-law grabbed my arm and started to pull it. She said, "We've got to get out of here." I wanted to go up to her and make sure she wasn't alive. She looked alive to me. I didn't want to leave. I wanted to stay there and decide how I felt. Somewhere, I still had faith she would just get up and be alive, but I was very upset and confused. I left and that was the last time I saw my daughter.

I don't know how much time any of this took. Time didn't exist. Everything I was dealing with was just inside of me. I wanted to scream and scream but I'm the kind of person who tries not to feel anything if lots of people are around. I wanted to be alone but was surrounded by people—doctors, my mother-in-law, strangers.

The hospital did an autopsy which said Beth died of a cerebral hemorrhage, but didn't say what caused it. After my doctor read the autopsy report, he said, "You don't owe me any money." There was no expression of sympathy, no nothing, just, "You don't owe me any money."

At home, I felt everybody I knew was going about their normal routines—talking about the groceries and stuff like that. People would say things to me like, "That's a nice dress." I was shocked that they could talk like that, that they could deal with other things besides Beth's death. I couldn't.

I had always been very aloof from my family. I never talked to my mother about anything. It was as if we had a wall between us. I was that way with most of the people in my life. I didn't have a funeral for Beth because I didn't want to cry in front of people and I knew there was no way I could stop myself. Some people feel if you don't have a funeral, you really don't care about the person who died, but I didn't feel there was any lack of respect. I felt if I had buried her somewhere, I would have been glued to that spot for the rest of my life. So we had her cremated and had her ashes dispersed over the ocean.

Jim didn't seem to understand why Beth's death affected me so much. He just threw himself into his work afterward and never said how he felt about it. But

I couldn't do anything at all. I sat in one place and stared at the walls for months. I felt angry that the world didn't care enough about children to spend money and make sure deaths like hers wouldn't happen. I thought millions of dollars were spent on killing people instead. And I was mad that doctors were just doing a business without getting close to their patients.

All I had wanted to be was a mother—to do sewing, cleaning, shopping. After Beth's death, I began to feel I had put too much of my life into my family and that was now dangerous for me. Staking so much on other people meant my stability depended on them, on whether my husband and our other child would stay alive. I knew I had to change my lifestyle. I didn't want to be Jim's wife any more. Because he still wanted to have the kind of marriage where I stayed home most of the time, eventually our relationship blew up and we separated.

My son, Steven, was four months old when Beth died. I didn't want to keep him after that. I loved him but I couldn't relate to him normally. It was too difficult for me to pick him up or talk to him. The sound of his voice reminded me too much of Beth's, and I felt I'd been through all of that emotional closeness before. I was afraid to get close to Steven and then lose him too.

While I fed him, bathed him, and changed him, I was more like a trained nurse than a mother. He began to go through some bad stages. He would rock in his sleep, banging his head against the wall and keeping me up all night. He would become fixated on things.

For hours, he would sit in one place and imitate the windshield wipers.

At three years old, he still couldn't talk. After Jim's family got upset, we took him to Stanford Hospital to see if he was retarded. They tested him and found he wasn't. But when people asked Steven to speak, he would bark like a dog. Looking back, it seems to me that was because he spent more time with the family dog than with me.

At four, he began to make other sounds. I could understand what he was saying but nobody else could. When Steven realized no one understood him, he refused to talk out loud but would only whisper to me or find some other way to communicate. For instance, in his pre-school, he wouldn't relate to the other children except by messing up their stuff. I didn't want him to go on to a public kindergarten because I thought they might treat him as if he were retarded.

After much searching, I found a private school which I felt would really work with him and give him a lot of attention. Until Steven started in kindergarten, I had never discussed Beth's death with anyone. I did then because I needed to give Steven's teacher some background information about his behavior.

I never told Steven about Beth's death, but he heard Jim's parents discuss it. I hadn't wanted to worry him. When I was a child, my mother told me about a baby she had had that died and it worried me. I became afraid I would die, too.

When Steven asked me about Beth, I answered him as lightly as possible because I didn't want to discuss it

> with him. As he gets older, I know I'll have to do that because I don't think it's something that should be hidden.

Time and again, people working with children find that young people are much more willing to come to grips with death than are adults. When we refuse to discuss death with them under the guise of protecting them, we need to realize that this is a pretense. It is we who are unwilling to confront death, not the children, And it is our ability to get past this, to discuss our feelings, thoughts, and fears about death, openly and honestly, that will allow our children to share how they feel about it as well. Once we do that, we may find ourselves inspired and strengthened by our children's experience of death.

When we choose to include children in the process of dealing with the death of a child, we need to speak to that child in a way that is both real for us and takes into consideration the child's age and level of understanding. References to heaven and angels are not appropriate to everyone's background and spiritual preferences. We may need to speak in stories and parables to young children, rather than in intellectual concepts. Too often, conceptualizing is a way of putting distance between us and our experience. And, in discussing death with children, we must leave some room for the child to have his or her own experience of death. Rather than say "This is how it is," we can say "This is how it is for me. It may or may not be this way for you."

After recognizing the need for communication with our children about the death of a sibling, we need to assess whether we can do the job alone or if we need support. If support is desired, we can look into family counseling or the services of organizations established to deal with the process of death and dying (please see section on organizations, p. 157).

## *Communication with Relatives and Friends*

"After my miscarriage, people would come up to me and say, 'You're lucky you're still young and you can have another child.' I wanted to kill them."

"When people used clichés with me, I found it very irritating. A priest visited us and said Ben's death was God's will. My wife's mother said, 'Congratulations. Now you have an angel in the family.' "

The above remarks from family members and friends seem blatantly inappropriate. However, within the context of a death, they are the norm rather than the exception. Most probably, at some time, we have said or thought we should say them ourselves.

We are all much better at avoiding pain than at letting things be. This behavior produces mechanical responses and trivial conversation: for instance, all of us can recall the knots of people seen at funerals discussing the weather or home redecorating in an attempt to ignore what has actually happened. Although such behavior is considered normal, it is not natural. Family and friends would probably like to offer what is best for the parent, but many are uncertain what this means and so try to come up with what they think will make the parent comfortable or make them feel better.

We should realize that on the occasion of a child's death, our social masks are stripped away and we are, perhaps, revealing ourselves for the first time without the faces we generally present outside the home. That means we don't care about "looking good," or about "being pleasant." We are showing parts of our personality relatives and friends have never seen.

In a sense, we have been rudely awakened from our dream life, but our friends and relatives may continue to be asleep. They may still be relating to us as we formerly related to them. We should not expect their lives to have been altered in the way ours has been. We should not expect them to suddenly be more open and honest. In fact, if a real sharing and communication is to take place, it is the parents who will have to take the initiative, perhaps at a time when we feel we shouldn't have to extend ourselves, when we believe someone else should handle that for us.

Often, the people around us become targets for the anger we feel over the fact that our child is dead. We begin to think that *their* insensitivity created our anger; we are angry because of what they said or didn't say; because they came at the wrong time or didn't show up at all.

Is there anything anyone could say to us that would really make a difference? That would be of assistance? Nurturing?

One mother said, "The friends I appreciated most were the ones who said, 'We know you hurt and we care for you. We don't know what to say, but we wanted to see you."

## *Support*

Historically, the family group or clan was the instrument of support for parents when a child died. That is generally not true today, and parents find themselves isolated and alone after such an experience.

John Golenski says, "In black and hispanic families there's a real sense of the clan coming in to support the parents in going through it. Grief is very openly shown by both sexes. And, almost always, members of poor, ethnic families want to see their dead child and to hold or touch his body.

"These people have a very clear structure of handling death. They know what they're supposed to do, how they're supposed to act, and who's supposed to do what. With black families, I have noticed a particular ritual. When the child's body is brought into the family room, someone, usually the mother's sister, takes the body from me or from the nurse and gives it to the mother, who grieves and speaks to the child. Then she hands it to the father, then the mother's mother, the father's mother, and so on through both sides of the dead child's family. Each person gets to hold the child and say their own good-bye. I think this really helps the people involved."

When lacking a closely knit, supportive family, we need to assemble support from others after a child's death. This could be our friends or groups and organizations that specifically deal with the death of a child.

In seeking support, it is a good idea to know what we want to be supported in. Are we looking for people who will pity us or for those who will allow us to continuously move though our grief? Are we surrounding ourself with people who want to make us feel comfortable or those who are willing to bear discomfort themselves?

Those who really support and serve us after a child's death are the people willing to go through the thick of it, to roll with the punches and hand out the tissues, to realize our anger has nothing to do with them although it may be directed at them.

People willing to be supportive at this time need to know it isn't a job for sissies or do-gooders (by that I mean people looking for a cosmic pat on the back for the nice things they do. Such a plan will never sustain them through the actual experience of supporting a bereaved parent). It takes guts and courage. It is an activity for warriors, for people willing to give up their comforts, to serve others without expectation. There are no merit badges given here and it is an environment within which all our wonderful philosophical contributions will be ignored or greeted with irritation. Nor is this a place to seek satisfaction. Rather one must bring satisfaction with him or her.

A staff member at the Shanti Project discussed with me some of the things their volunteer grief counselors are told. "The first things a griever needs to know is that he or she isn't crazy. It's important for our volunteers to honor the various styles of response to grieving, to not place on these people their own expectations or criteria for successful coping. Anyway, I think many of our standards come from T.V. shows in which people go through enormous, world-shaking difficulties, yet manage to resolve them in twenty-eight minutes. We also need to realize some grievers will resolve these issues faster than we think they should.

"Our volunteers also need to know that grief can be an extremely disorienting experience and that the tendency of the counselor might be to respond to the griever as being different, alien, frightening, and unbalanced."

Most likely, we have nothing brilliant to tell a person whose child has just died, at least, nothing that will be initially listened to. If we really do have something worthwhile to say, we need to hold it for the right moment. We should know nothing we say will make it better, and anything we have to offer to deaden the pain—whether it be a verbal palliative, a drink, or a drug—will only prolong the agony. The only way through this experience is through it.

Supporting a parent does not mean agreeing with them and it doesn't mean disagreeing with them. Both of these are simply additions to what the parent already has to deal with. For instance, agreeing that life is unfair just increases the rut. Disagreeing, saying that life really isn't unfair, invites them to double their efforts to get across their point of view. The more we resist, the more they will cling. So, support means just to be. If we can be there for someone else, allowing them to be and allowing to pass through us whatever is given, we create an environment in which there is room to move on, a supportive environment.

"When a person is in fresh grief," says Stephen Levine, "they just have to be in fresh grief. If you're sharing that with someone, you'll start to see parts of yourself that you haven't seen before. If people are in an atmosphere that allows them to be themselves and doesn't offer a model for how they should or shouldn't grieve, they'll come through all right, without getting stuck. There'll be a time when enough is enough and they will let go of their grief more and more."

In supporting others, we need to construct our own support system where we can discharge, rather than suppress, our emotions. People working with dying children and/or their parents open themselves to tremendous loss. Those who stick with it do so because of the opportunity for growth and satisfaction. In order to avoid debilitation, many of them use support networks or counseling resources.

"When a child I've been counseling dies, I feel a real personal sense of loss," said Judy Conley. "That hasn't lessened through the years, though I've worked with more and more people. However, that doesn't make me want to avoid my work. For me, these deep feelings of sadness are as much a part of my life as feelings of great joy. I'm glad to be able to feel all of it and know it's all part of being human."

Gail Perrin, a clinical nurse specializing in oncology, started working with children cancer patients in 1966.

"There weren't any tremendous advances in pediatric cancer then and, the first year, I dealt with about twelve children dying of malignancies. I noticed nobody ever wanted to take care of these families because they seemed too difficult to deal with and, being the new staff nurse, I was assigned to them. This was, at the same time, painful and extremely fortuitous for me because I was able to get to know them, and they were such special people.

"Death is a release for many of the children I've worked with. By that time, their lives have so little quality to them that no matter how sad I am to see them go, I somehow shift from my own needs to the needs of the child to be released from an extremely painful situation. I wouldn't have them stay alive and face the physical and emotional pain that often accompany terminal illness.

"To me, the aspect of my work that outweighs everything else is in being able to be with a parent who feels he or she not only did everything they could for their child but did it well, to see the successful resolution of their grief and the growth it has produced. While, on the other hand, it may look like my job requires me to be involved in a constantly sorrowful situation, what's actually available is an amazing richness from all the growth going on, and the sense that I have had a part in it."

If we are committed to reentering life and moving through a child's death, it is wise to enlist people who will support us in doing this.

Our part of the bargain is to make ourselves be supportable, to continue communicating even if what we need to communicate is that we want to shut down.

After the death of a child, we are not easy to be with and we should know this. We are responsible for making ourselves amenable to support. People's support is a gift and no one owes it to us.

# *Setting Up a Support Group*

When no support group exists in our area, we may choose to start one. There are several basic aims to keep in mind when starting such a group: What is the purpose? What results do we want to produce? How do we contact other parents?

The following are examples of two organizations established for parents whose children died. One is a parent support group; the other, a grief counseling organization, set up not just for parents.

Bob Murnane runs a support group for parents at Santa Rosa Memorial Hospital.

"A parent had been through a seminar the hospital held concerning mourning. She wanted something more. At the time, I was working with a nurse in pediatrics and we were also interested in providing a group for bereaved parents. Our intentions became focused when this parent showed up.

"The hospital was willing to provide us room to hold our meetings. I did some public relations and let people know about the group through local radio and TV programs. Parents and health professionals responded, wanting to participate.

"One of the elements we decided on was that this wasn't going to be a therapy group. Another was that the parents in the group needed to be responsible for organizing the group and making sure it happened. They would also have to come up with topics for discussion.

"The people in our group are very open to newcomers.

Sometimes, people coming into the group are very angry and even hostile. But the core group has also waited, giving these people time to feel comfortable about being here, and eventually they opened up and became part of the group."

The Marin County Grief Counseling program provides free, short-term, individual, family, or group bereavement counseling for local residents. This group is an offshoot of the Marin Suicide Prevention program and works with the local coroner's office.

"When starting such a program," said Joan Sheldon, the program's director, "you must be very patient. If you can enlist the backing of the coroner's office or a political official, you can then lend credence to your program."

When a death occurs in Marin County, the survivors of that death are offered this service. For anticipated deaths, notification comes from the County Office of Vital Statistics in the form of a phone call. In the case of sudden, unexpected death, a letter and Grief Counseling brochure is sent from the County Coroner's office when the death certificate is issued.

When someone requests counseling, a team of two trained volunteers are matched to the case. They arrange a meeting place and time with the client. What usually occurs is eight weekly counseling sessions, each one to two hours long.

"The people we train as counselors don't have to be psychiatrists. They do, however, have to be separated enough from their own grief to be able to counsel and to be in touch enough with their own feelings to let people into their lives."

Very often, accounts of the death of a child include descriptions of insensitivity displayed by doctors, nurses, and other medical personnel. In cases of sudden death, parents are often separated from their children, to wait unaccompanied in sterile rooms. In a terminal illness, many times the doctor who has been closely attending a child-patient will suddenly disappear when death is imminent. Similarly, staff people who have been with the child for weeks or months will become unavailable.

Rather than offer the support and patience parents often require after a child's death, hospital staff members are often curt and businesslike with them, dispensing drugs or giving out the necessary papers, not willing to give of themselves.

Medical personnel, especially doctors, are no better at dealing with death than the rest of us, but because their positions are highly respected and we have made them into our *shamans*, investing them with power over life and death, we somehow expect them to have mastered sensitivity in this area.

"Physicians are the brahmans of our society," says John Golenski. "They represent, quintessentially, what we consider to be human. They are 'paragons of success,' and highly rewarded materially for the work they do.

"Young physicians and med students have an inordinate fear of death, more so than the average person. And yet, they are the people invested with having control over death, with the tools to deal with death. Because they do seem to save a lot of people from, at least, a particular occasion of death, it creates for them, and for the people who use their services an illusion of power to create immortality. Death is certainly seen as a failure for them and tends to undercut their position."

Marty Enriquez, a hospital employee and coordinator of a hospital-supported program for parents who have suffered a neonatal death, adds that physicians hardly know how to deal with death, particularly the obstetricians. "They seem to take it as a personal affront when one of their patients dies. In relation to our program, often doctors don't want the parents of their former patients counseled. Some have requested that our brochures be hidden and referrals to our program be made only through the doctors themselves."

Hospital deaths, so commonplace today, were an exception until the end of the eighteenth century. Up till then, most people died at home, surrounded by parents, friends, and neighbors. At the end of the eighteenth century, however, doctors discovering the principles of hygiene complained about the overcrowded conditions of deathbed vigils and urged their patients to go to hospitals. Considerations for the patient's spiritual and emotional well-being began to be superceded by attention to his or her physical condition.

The death of a child when handled insensitively by medical staff members not only creates greater problems for the grieving parents but also produces stress for the staff members, who either have to justify their behavior or suppress any memory of it. This affects their own well-being and ability to function in their profession. It is to the advantage of parents and hospital personnel for doctors and nurses to begin to include in their training provisions for relating to parents of children who have died in a human and empathetic manner, in a way that elevates everyone, rather than demeans all parties, in a way in which the grief is shared rather than covered over.

Why should medical personnel open themselves to the experience of grief? Because they can either go through the experience or suppress it; either deal with it or pretend it doesn't exist. It just doesn't disappear. The sooner hospital staffs talk about the stresses inherent in their relating with dying children and their parents, the sooner we can all work on alleviating these stresses in everyone.

Some hospitals are beginning to create programs that deal with the issues of death and dying. Canada's Victoria Hospital Corporation, for example, has established programs for parents of children who die in their neonatal intensive care unit and the staff members who work with these children.

When the death of a child seems inevitable, the hospital's protocol for parents includes giving them the chance and sometimes encouraging them to hold and touch their child, even if on a respirator; take pictures of their child; discuss funeral arrangements openly and honestly; be present at the time of death; hold and touch their child after death, in private; bathe their child after death.

Group sessions in which death is talked about are set up for nurses on this unit. The goals of these sessions is to encourage the nurses to become aware of stress and allow for appropriate expressions or reactions to the stress; discuss how avoiding talking about death can stultify the natural grief process; discuss grief reactions; discover how society rewards inappropriate grieving and learn how to recognize and discourage such reactions; consider the impact of their protocol; share ideas for future development of their programs for parent and staff support.

Programs such as these, when entered into willingly and wholeheartedly, are a step toward reversing the trend of medical institutions toward greater reliance on technical sophistication and less emphasis on the quality of life. Such programs may, in fact, provide medical personnel with an experience of the great contribution they can actually make in the lives of the children and parents they interact with.

## *Contribution:*

A condition of giving along with others; supply or furnish a share to.

## *Completion:*

A condition of wholeness or perfection.

*MARTHA:*
The first two years after my son was diagnosed with leukemia, I went through a lot of anger. I was angry at God. But still, I felt one should let things happen as they happen and continue to talk about it, not shut down. We talked a lot about it in our family and we went through what there was to go through. Because we wanted our son to have as much support as possible, we took him to the Center for Attitudinal Healing,

where there was a group of children he could share with, a group he could really belong to. As he came closer to his death, and the medicine no longer worked, we let him choose between staying in the hospital or being at home. He came home and the people from the center would visit us there.

By the time he died, I accepted his death. Oh, it bothered me a lot. Every morning I cried, but I still felt that life goes on. So while I experienced a lot of emotional havoc, I also was able to watch myself go through it all. The whole family cried together, acknowledged one another, cared, and worked it out of our systems.

What really inspired me was the kind of support my son had received from the Center for Attitudinal Healing. I wanted to start a branch of this group where I lived so it would be available here. I knew, though, I didn't want to do that until I was complete in my own process.

My son died at the end of May. By October, I felt my process was complete and began making the initial phone calls for the organization I eventually started.

When the process is complete—when a child's death has been accepted; when we have moved through the emotional upheaval, the mental gymnastics, the physical stress; when we have said all there is to say and allowed ourselves to be supported in saying it—the element that completes the cycle is contribution. Certainly, those who have entered upon this path have a great contribution to make. They exist as proof of the indomitability of the human spirit. They have withstood the tests of fire and ice. They are transformed. Some people make their contribution to the general public; some make it to their families and friends; some in the areas of death and dying; some in the fields in which they are interested.

*ANN:*

There are only nine minutes I cannot account for, when I was on the phone. I had put my daughter down for her morning nap and when I went into her room, I knew instantly what had happened. She was blue . . . face down on the mattress.

I picked her up and began artificial respiration. Then I scooped her up in my arms and started for the front door to yell for my neighbor. My four-year-old son was watching cartoons and I told him to stay put.

My neighbor put her on the floor and rebreathed her while I called my husband, the ambulance, and the doctor. Twice, while dialing the ambulance, I got the wrong number.

As she lay on the floor, her blue color began to be replaced by pink as the oxygen went in.

My doctor arrived at the hospital just seconds after we did. My daughter was put on a complete life support system. Then the doctor examined her and said it had been a sudden infant death syndrome incident. He said her EEG was virtually flat and that there was neither heartbeat nor respiration. I said I wanted to see her before they took her off the systems, and as I walked through her door, she began to breathe on her own.

Then they got a heartbeat. My doctor said, "The decision has been made for us. We'll put her into intensive care."

The specialists were very kind. At no time did they want to give us false hope. A friend of mine sent for a minister. I told him, "If God can't grant me a miracle and give her back to me whole, I'd rather He take her home." I thought getting her back whole was a lot to ask and maybe it was something we weren't entitled to.

I ran into my Lamaze teacher who happened to be in the hospital. When she asked what I was doing there, I started crying. She stayed with us a long time.

We stayed through the night, watching and waiting. They gave her oxygen support to keep the oxygen level high. When we got home, we made arrangements for our son to sleep out again and returned to the hospital. My daughter's blood pressure had dropped and she had been given a transfusion.

My emotions ran the gamut. I wondered why this was happening to me. Why was someone created with so much love being taken from me? I felt shortchanged.

The next day she had a cardiac arrest and died. When the doctor found us, I could tell what he was going to say before he spoke. My husband didn't connect things. The resident, whom we had never seen before, said to him, "The baby's dead."

My husband went gray. I stood crying and asked to see her. We walked back to the intensive care nursery where they had taken her off the machines and wrapped her in a pink blanket. I looked at her, stroked her hair, told her how much we loved her and how sorry we were. My husband did the same. The head nurse held my husband in her arms and cried with him. Their support of us made the whole thing easier to bear. But walking out, knowing there was no going back, knowing I would now have to tell the rest of the family, was difficult.

The supervisor of nursing came in and said, "You know, you're going to have to make some kind of arrangement," and suggested the name of a local funeral home. By then, anything would do. We were in shock. As we were leaving, I met my obstetrician in the hall. He hadn't known about the baby and when I told him, all he could say was, "My baby. My baby."

The funeral home was very inexpensive. They took care of everything that we couldn't handle at that point, including writing down a list of things we needed to bring to the funeral. I knew all the arrangements would have to be made before my parents arrived as I knew they couldn't cope with it at all.

Telling my son was very hard. He had been in the middle of a very stressful two days—what with the police and fire department coming to the house, being sent away to friends. When we returned from the hospital, he wanted to know how his sister was. It was tough explaining things to a four-year-old who had never experienced a death before, not even a pet's death. I also knew he would have a difficult time grasping the idea of sudden infant death syndrome. But I plowed on and told him she had died of an illness with that name.

For months, when my son and I were driving places, he would lean over the back seat and say, right into my ear, "Why did she die?" Then I would go through the whole thing again with him. He would ask, "Why didn't she breathe?" "What's a disease?" "Can I get one?"

Two years later, he was still coming to me with questions about his sister's death. Sometimes he would say, "I was just thinking about my sister." And I would tell him that was good and that she was a very treasured part of our memory. I'd also let him know that my husband and I still thought of her.

Something we did as soon as we got home from the hospital was to take apart my daughter's nursery. We cleaned it out and turned it back into the guest room it had originally been. I wanted to have this done, too, before my folks got in. I didn't want to do this with anyone but my husband. I didn't want anybody else going through her things. Doing that was extremely painful. We just put her things into barrels until we could dispose of them.

My parents stayed with us three weeks. People around us tried as hard as they could to take care of us and when I saw people who couldn't handle the death I took care of them. Everyone wanted to do something for us but very few were equipped to lend us the emotional support we needed.

My husband and I have always turned to each other first, and at this time, we needed to be very close. We hung on to each other physically and emotionally, having to be intertwined all the time. My husband's company was extremely sympathetic and gave him as much time off as he felt he needed.

My son became the only reason for me to get up in the morning. He wanted to keep to his routine and didn't understand the chaotic condition of our lives. He, of course, still needed and wanted our support and wanted us to be interested in him. For a while, I felt I led two lives. In one, I was grieving. In the other, I was performing a mother's duties.

In the town in which we live, a nurse will come within forty-eight hours of a SIDS death to talk with you. She brought information on crib death and told me if I needed someone to talk to she would come by again.

I began having flashbacks of my child's death. They were like seeing a movie and would happen regardless of where I was or what I was doing: I could be eating dinner, talking to someone, anything. My doctor explained these images as my mind's safety valve, a way of cleaning out the cobwebs. Eventually, they began to fade.

My friends put me in touch with the local sudden infant death syndrome group. Members began sending me letters telling me how sorry they were and asking me to contact them if I needed help. About six weeks after the death, my husband and I went to our first meeting.

When we got there, and I saw women standing around, laughing and joking, I told my husband, "How can they laugh? I'll never laugh again in my whole life."

One woman had lost her child a year before. She was pregnant again and happy about it. Another had lost hers five years before. One had gone through a SIDS death eleven years before. Just seeing she was well adjusted and happy was like seeing the light at the end of the tunnel. I liked that.

As I got further and further away from my daughter's death, my wounds began to heal. In the beginning, my heart would stop every time I saw a baby dressed the way she had been dressed. I was almost afraid to turn on the daytime TV for fear of seeing baby product ads. The first time I picked up a baby after mine died, I noticed how good it felt and how my arms had ached for a baby.

I became very involved with the SIDS group. After attending four meetings, I was invited to a board meeting and found there was a need for a representative where I lived. I was asked how I would feel talking to parents who had just lost their children. Though I felt very hesitant, I remembered how desperately I had wanted to talk with people who had been through a SIDS death. I agreed to be the parent-contact person in my area.

The parent group I had joined continued to meet once a month. It was a self-help organization, and we tried to have a pediatrician or public health specialist at every meeting, to talk about current SIDS research. I became part of a team, working with a doctor, a public health nurse, and a coroner who would speak with newly bereaved parents whose children died of SIDS.

The first personal letter I wrote to a parent I didn't

> know was very difficult, but I was able to draw on those things people had said which meant a lot to me after my daughter's death.
>
> I found that getting involved in this way gave me a sense that my child hadn't died for nothing. And that if I could help one person through the incident, in a certain way her death was justified and could be of some use.

In order to contribute, we must come to realize that the wound can be licked only so much and that attention to our personal processes can be taken past the point of being worthwhile into a realm of selfish absorption, in other words, a dead end.

To move on, we need to become detached from the endless fascination with our personal needs and desires and begin to develop an interest in others so that we can distribute all we have received.

# 5

"The child will always be there. Real love doesn't die. It's the physical body that dies. Genuine, authentic love has no expectations whatsoever; it doesn't even need the physical presence of a person. . . . Even when he is dead and buried that part of you that loves the person will always live. What happens to the physical body does not diminish that love."

—Elisabeth Kübler-Ross*

We have always had accounts of the survival of the being after death. However, these reports were usually considered to be within the ken of religious experience or mysticism and people seemed divided into two categories with regard to them. As with UFOs, you either believe it or you don't. With hard, scientific research now being done in the domain of human consciousness (such

*Reprinted from *Psychology Today* Magazine, copyright © 1976 Ziff Davis Publishing Co.

as psychokinesis and Kirlian photography, which captures auras on film), it is highly possible empirical evidence of life-after-death will be produced.

*JEANNE:*

We were down in California and Evan was up at our home in Alaska. He had come for our youngest child's birth, and then decided to go back up and build a cabin about seventeen miles from ours, live in the mountains alone, and do a kind of "walkabout." He had been going to school in California and spending his summers in Alaska but now he wanted to be there as a way of life. He felt he had enough school for a while. He was seventeen.

Since he'd been a child, Evan had had a muscle-bone involvement for which doctors had no answer. When whatever it was left his spine, his spine became quite rigid. At this time of his life, it was in his hands and all of his joints were very swollen. He had the feeling it wouldn't be long before he no longer could use his body the way he wanted. In fact, he had had premonitions he would not live to be twenty. When he was fifteen, and had broken a thighbone and was in a body cast, he had gone into a deep depression. I finally told him, "You've just got to talk about this and tell me what's happening." And, between clenched teeth, he said he felt he was going to die young and he hoped it was just his age or the accident that was making him feel that way.

But he lived in a way in which he had to do what he wanted to do. Growing up in Alaska, he had lived with the cycles of the land and the wild animals. Right then, he had to go north.

My husband, Greg, felt a lot of anxiety about Evan being in Alaska. He wanted to send in a helicopter to make sure he was all right. I was against it and felt it would violate what Evan had gone to do. He planned to stay there all winter, trap, and live by himself. He left in April and built the cabin. Once a month, he would return to our home by the lake, pick up mail, and get supplies.

Our foster son, Rick, joined him for a while. I had called the mail pilot to see if Rick could bring us back a small tent, but when he picked up Rick he didn't have time to get the tent and so Evan said he would prepare the tent the next day.

The people staying in our house saw Evan go out with one of our boats to the middle of the lake to see if he could see the plane. Our rule about using the boats was always to stay away from the middle of the lake when the water was too cold to survive in. In general, people kept that rule, although Greg and I broke it occasionally.

When the people in the cabin looked out, they saw Evan in the water in the middle of the lake. It seemed he had sat on one of the canoe's struts, which had broken in half and catapulted him into the water. He had fallen into the lake with his heavy boots on and no life jacket. He held onto the canoe in order to kick his way to shore.

One man plunged into save him but turned back because of the temperature of the water. Our other two boats had been borrowed and were six miles away. On the shore, people tried to make a raft but there was no dry wood. They cut down green trees which sunk as soon as they were pushed into the water. In the meantime, Evan had gotten closer to shore in the half hour that had elapsed but, eventually, he was gone. They were amazed he could have held on so long with the cold the way it was and his fingers in the condition they were in.

The people in the cabin would have had to walk twenty-five miles to send us a letter about what had happened. I think the trauma prevented them. Anyway, their attitude was that Evan was gone and there was nothing they could do.

During that time, I would find myself walking with Rose, our new baby, and saying to her, "Don't leave us, honey. Don't leave us." Then I would think, "What's wrong with me?" I also began having dreams that there was a bear up north in the shadows. I had written to Evan about this.

Two months after it happened, I received a letter about it. It was the day after Thanksgiving and I had Rose in a pack on my back at the post office. I opened the letter right there. The fellow who wrote it started off talking about the events of the morning it happened. Gradually, I could tell what he was going to say. I went out of the post office saying, "My God!"

A man stopped and asked if he could help me. I told him, "My son is dead." He asked if he could drive me home. I sat in his car but it wouldn't start. I just sat there, not crying, stunned. Finally he said, "It won't start," and my senses began to return. I told him I wanted to walk and took the path through the woods.

My immediate response was to start talking to Evan. I felt he was right there and that this was a choice he had made. It was hard for me to understand why he had made that choice.

I had never thought about death very much, even though we lived close to it in Alaska and the land could have taken any of us at any time. Evan and I were very, very close. Because the three of us had lived in such isolation, I had been his playmate and he had been a very deep companion for me. Sometimes, I had felt as if he were the adult and I the child. Adolescence was a bit different. He had struggled to get free of our relationship, which I had understood. When he left for the north alone, I felt as if, most of the time, we were standing back from each other.

When Greg came home, I told him. He did not experience any part of Evan as being alive and it was very hard on him. He just felt the loss and tragedy and carried a lot of guilt over it. He thought he hadn't been tough enough in establishing safety patterns with the boats, and that's why Evan drowned.

There were times when I was very high, overwhelmed by joy and a sense of freedom. I had tremendous gratitude for all that the three of us had shared. I realized that those things which are most important we were never going to lose. I was still in contact with the things I loved most about Evan—his spirit, the essence of his being. His body was gone but our relationship was still very much alive. I began to feel that, perhaps, everything we love is eternal for us and death can't take it away.

Obviously, there were other moments when that high experience was not there, when it seemed my relationship with him was just imagination and that I had really lost him forever. So his death brought me to a crisis between my everyday reality (or daytime reality) and another (or nighttime) reality. In the latter, everything was possible. In the former, I scoffed at all that.

I felt as if Evan were around us all the time, watching what we were doing. Having made his own adjustment to passing over, he was very interested in helping us with ours and in making us aware he was not dead but there beside us.

I knew there was a gap between my two realities and I couldn't bear going from one to the other. I saw that unless I closed that gap, I would lose Evan. I made a commitment to totally accepting the reality of his aliveness.

Greg thought I might be trying to escape from reality. He was a very rational man who believed that humans were locked into their physical form which had led them, as a species, into a cul-de-sac, like the dinosaurs, from which we could never get out. He was very despairing about that. Of my experience with Evan, he said, "I don't want to take that away from you. Probably, you're more right about it than I am. I just don't experience it."

It was his decision to locate some psychic mediums to see if their experience of Evan coincided with mine. I was reluctant to do that because I didn't want to have to validate my experience through others, but I felt Greg needed that and so I agreed.

We went to a medium in Santa Barbara. It was strange. We had never been involved with anything like that before. He told me Evan wanted me to stop worrying about my figure. I got very angry with this and said, "My son is dead and you're telling me he doesn't want me to worry about my figure." But I realized, this response was appropriate. It had been an issue between Evan and me. The way the medium described Evan was very down to earth and was the way I had been relating to him. It was as if this person, who had passed over, was basically the same personality, although he was going through some things which were very hard for him to communicate to us. The medium told us Evan wanted us to find his watch and wear it. We wrote to the people in our cabin asking if they knew anything about this watch, which he had usually worn. They found it in our cabin. He'd left it on the table.

We also went to an English medium who gave us a lot of evidence of Evan. These things made a tremendous transformation possible for Greg, especially the idea of the survival of the personality after death. He had new hope for the world and for man. Life after death meant for him there was more to life than just a physical body and brain. He felt that man's hope was in expanding his consciousness and he wanted to work for man's transition into that way of being.

When Evan's presence was around, he would give

Greg and me a physical signal. It felt like a tiny insect or an electrical current going across our foreheads and down the bridges of our noses. Sometimes, Greg and I would be miles apart and get that signal at the same time. I think Evan worked really hard at giving us evidence of his survival.

One night I was alone in my house with Rose, and was feeling very uncomfortable. Sometimes, when Evan's presence was around, it would seem as if there were a peeping tom prowling around. I took Rose upstairs and turned the radio on loud. The music was "The Nutcracker Suite." Rose started jumping off and on the bed again and again. She began saying, "Watch this, Evan. Watch this." Although Evan died when she was a baby, she had always related to him as if he were alive. Occasionally, she would say he was smiling at her.

One summer at the lake in Alaska, Rose was including Evan in her games a lot. A friend took a boat ride with her one day. When they got to shore and were returning to the house, Rose was behind him and he heard her say, "Well, maybe he can see you now, Evan." When the friend saw me, he said, "Jeanne, did Evan stand with one shoulder lower than the other?" He exactly imitated Evan's way of standing. It sent chills through me because he had never seen Evan. He told me that after he'd heard Rose, he turned around and there was a young man standing near her who lifted his hand in greeting.

After Evan's death, Greg had premonitions about his own death. I rejected these. We had Rose and a new baby was on the way. When we were rushing to complete our film about Alaska, he told me, "I have to get the music and narration done, because then you can finish it without me."

In a way, Evan's death was a tremendous gift to Greg. He began to dream of his own death as if he would just pass through a way and it would be all right.

In 1977, three years after Evan's death, Greg died in a plane crash. For a while, after this, I lost contact with Evan. I had had to put a lot of energy into the other children and get our lives in order. I now feel I am in communication with both Greg and Evan. I experience my ties with both of them. Although I miss having them here physically, I experience their deaths as part of a plan that we have all agreed to and in which we all have our roles.

# 6

Three people I have had the good fortune to spend time with I consider experts in both the philosophical and practical sides of death. They are all involved in the work of bringing great numbers of people to an awareness of themselves, but this is not why I have chosen these people. I picked them because of their qualities of dedication to humanity, compassion, and especially because of their simplicity and naturalness. Interviews with Yogiraj Sri Swami Satchidananda, Brother David Steindl-Rast, and Rebbe Zalman Schachter follow.

## *Yogiraj Sri Swami Satchidananda*

Whatever comes will go. Whatever goes will come. When we get something, we may have to lose it one day.

The purpose of a body is so it can be used by a being as a vehicle, somewhat like how we use an automobile.

To fulfill desires, beings need vehicles. Once those

desires have been fulfilled—experienced—with the help of a body, the being leaves that body.

But why should beings lose their bodies as children within a short time of getting that particular body? Probably, within that period, the being has fulfilled certain desires. If a desire is such that it can be experienced within a short period of time, the being will use it for that length of time: a day, a few months, a few years; and then leave that body.

To give you an analogy: Suppose you are riding in a comfortable car and you then decide to go into a very rough jungle area. Obviously, your comfortable car will be of little use in the jungle and so you switch to a jeep. Your occupancy in the car and your occupancy in the jeep were for a specific purpose. When you finish that job, you get something which is appropriate to whatever job is next. We use bodies in the same way.

Parents should know that ultimately their children do not belong to them. Children are totally independent souls. In fact, they choose their parents. It is not the other way around. Parents are only temporary caretakers. They provide the beings with a body.

When the child leaves its body—says good-bye—the parents have finished their jobs. They were able to serve the soul and should then allow it to go on to further experiences, instead of trying to possess that soul for themselves. They should wish that soul peace and joy, unending happiness, and liberation.

When one truly understands and accepts this, they don't spend time feeling sad and being unable to fulfill their other duties. Sorrow is due to ignorance of what is really happening, of what a being truly is.

I don't mean to say that when one loses a child they should be happy. However, they should know they have done their job. And they should also know that the soul is immortal. It never dies. The truth is very simple, but when we are not aware of it, it is hard to accept.

In any event, can a parent bring a child back by feeling sad? If people cry too much for the soul, they continuously pull it back and do not allow it to go out for further work. This is similar to the kind of parent who will not let his child leave home to go away to school. Such action creates a block, a brake to the child.

The soul, observing its parents' actions, might feel, "I am free. I have been promoted. I don't know why these people are crying so much. They are not losing me because they have never owned me. They just did their job." Such souls may even pray for their parents' peace.

We simply do our part and when our part is over, the soul goes on.

Swami Satchidananda is the founder of the Integral Yoga Institute with centers in the United States, Europe, and India. He is the author of several books, including *Integral Yoga Hatha* and *Beyond Words*. Active in the ecumenical movement, he has spoken at the United Nations and has met with many world spiritual leaders.

## *Brother David Steindl-Rast*

Why do beings lose their bodies as children? Why do beings lose their bodies at any age? What does it mean to lose one's body? Is there still a loser after that loss? And can that which is lost still be called a body? How could beings like us answer questions like these? How can anybody speak about being without any body and make sense? What does anybody know about having a body, let alone getting or losing it?

It may seem strange to start answering one question by raising half a dozen more. Yet, it might take ten times as many to cut through dualistic notions which prove simply inadequate when confronted with reality. The one who speaks of having a body cannot deny being a body, somebody. And this is not merely a play on words. It's a reality which can no longer be overlooked "when a body meets a body coming through the rye." Overlooking our full bodily reality in asking the questions can at best lead to half-truths in giving answers. Half-truths are more manageable of course than life in its full complexity. That's why they are so tempting.

In reality, I must hold on to both poles of the truth and maintain the creative tension between having and being a body. I realize myself by putting my body where my convictions are. According to my convictions, I make choices—choosing my partner for bodily intimacy, my side in political demonstrations. These choices presuppose a body, but they presuppose more than a body. If there is no body, nobody will realize any convictions, realize them in the double sense of becoming aware and putting into practice (and these two are inseparable). And yet, unlike the body, convictions are not limited by space and time. I realize myself by "becoming somebody," as we say, but in so doing I go beyond what is merely bodily. I touch the horizon of space, the horizon of time, but I do so in time and space, in the body.

Once we go beyond dualistic half-truths concerning our life in the body, we achieve a different focus of questioning when somebody dies, a more realistic one. More humble, too, and more compassionate.

The mother who has lost her child is not concerned with theoretical speculations. Somebody she loved is dead. A body that was part of her own body is a corpse. In the words of the Bible: "A voice is heard in Ramah, lamentation, bitter weeping; Rachel weeping for her children will not be comforted, for her children are no more." (Jeremiah 31:15). They are no more and she will not be comforted, for they are no more. No fine theories will make these tiny toes wiggle again. No pious thoughts will make these staring eyes move and shine again.

C. S. Lewis raises this problem in his novel *Perelandra*. It is a problem with which death always confronts us, but above all the death of a child. Nothing makes us more forcefully face the question of meaning than a life which so obviously remains an unfulfilled promise. But does any life, do all lives together, begin to exhaust the promise life seems to hold?

When confronted with something apparently so planless, apparently so meaningless as the death of a child, we must choose. The choice is between trying to explain, or else to simply suffer through. To "explain" means to flatten out in a two-dimensional picture or diagram what in reality is multidimensional. Explanation is therefore always a half-truth. Access to the full truth is life lived. We start where we are. We set our eyes on one movement, the one in which we are already engaged. We rage, we howl in our bereavement, we exhaust our grief, we savour the bittersweet flavor of our own grieving, feel the throbbing of our scars and the delicious fatigue that comes with slow healing. By being content with this one movement, our own, we miss nothing, for it will lead us into the master movement. The moment we decide to be, rather than explain, we understand, for we no longer try to stand over against that which is.

Clearly, the decision "to be" is a religious decision. It is *the* religious decision, if you want. Paradoxically, it has everything and nothing to do with any formal religion. Everything, because formal religion has no other justification but to give this decision form. Nothing, because it does not depend on formal religion, which sometimes even provides an unintentional shelter from having to make that basic religious decision. But to make the decision *to be* means finding the center, the heart, one's own and that of all there is, for the two are one. It means finding God, if one wants to use that name.

But there is one more dualism we must overcome, the dualism between finding and seeking the center. Paradoxically again, it is only in the security of having found the center that we can dare risk seeking it again and again. The death of a child raises questions to which no answer is imaginable. We have decided "to be" and so have entered into the plan; we have discovered the center within our own heart; and only in the strength of this position can we admit, "There seems no plan because it is all plan: there seems no center because it is all center."

Images like those I have evoked here might nourish our inner life long before an acute crisis such as we envisaged arises. Poetic images are high power food for our spiritual journey, and we will be well advised to include poetry among our essential provisions. But poetic images do not explain. On the contrary, they enable us to live with unexplained reality in all its rich fullness.

Nothing I have shared is meant as material for counseling in the hour of bereavement. To take it as such would mean a complete misunderstanding. The one who offers eloquent advice to people struck dumb by the impact of death reminds me all too painfully of an undertaker who seizes the same opportunity for an effective sales pitch on grave plots and expensive coffins. To "be with"—in silence most likely—will in most cases be far more compassionate than any form of counseling, no matter how well intentioned.

Even God, as conceived in the Bible, neither gives nor promises to give good advice in the hour of crisis. What the God of compassion, of suffering-with, promises to the one who "abides under the shadow of the Almighty" is this: "I will be with him in the midst of his troubles." (Psalms 91:15). Nourishing our understanding of what it's all about beforehand—and it's never too soon—will help us find our place, find the thread and the center, when the crisis comes.

Brother David Steindl-Rast is a Franciscan friar who has been a student of Buddhism and has taught in many places, including Naropa Institute in Boulder, Colorado.

# Zalman M. Schachter

Why do children die? Any generalization about this is absurd.

In certain instances, there are souls that make their way down to earth and somehow don't have the stamina necessary to continue on this plane. But because they're stubborn, they're given the choice to try it. This choice is given to them by "The Court from on High." The best way I can define this is by saying this court is composed of all the beings in charge of destiny. Every soul has a different committee.

So, for example, a soul says, "I've got to try it." The committee says, "Listen, you tried it before. It didn't work out." The soul says, "This time I'll be grounded." Then the soul gets into a womb and can't stand it. Earlier memories come back which the soul can't take and it leaves.

I've known a number of women who've had spontaneous abortions and in talking to them, they've said things like, "I was angry when the baby decided to leave. When I became pregnant again, that soul was hanging around, wanting to come back, and I didn't want it at all. I said, 'You didn't keep your words last time so I want someone else.' "

There are other cases. Once there was a Hasidic master who was shown his children just before they were circumcised. His children didn't live very long after that. When his wife was about to have another baby, she went to a great master and asked why her children didn't stay with her, why they seemed unhappy with her. The master told her that everything would be fine if she didn't show her husband the baby until after he was circumcised. When the child was born and her husband wanted to see him, the mother wouldn't allow it. She kept it away until a month after the circumcision and then showed it to him. He looked at the child and said, "Nicer ones than you, I've sent back." So in this case, you had a very powerful parent who figured before he would invest himself in a soul, raise it, and mix with its *karma*, he wanted to be sure it was the right one.

The *Baal Shem Tov* (the founder of the Hasidic movement) promised a woman she would have a baby after years of no children. The baby was born, lived two years, and died. The woman was very angry, and went to the Baal Shem Tov and asked, "Why did you give me such a child if you knew it was going to die?"

He told her, "There was a great holy being who converted to Judaism. He had been able to clean up everything he had done in one incarnation except the first two years of his life. When he came to Heaven, he was allotted a space lower than what he could have gotten if he'd worked out those two years. When you asked for a child, this soul was waiting to have two years with a certain kind of mother, one who practiced her religion. He came down and did the first two years with you. You have been able to give so much to this holy being."

She went away happy.

The issue of reincarnation is very complex. It contains the idea of completing something. This is true even in the death of children. Something is completed, although it has a tragic form.

Rabbi Yitzhak Luria, "The Holy Lion," attended a wedding of a bride and groom who were very, very holy people. After the wedding ceremony, the couple went to have their first meal together in privacy, which is the Jewish custom: it is the moment to form a bond after the public wedding. These two began eating and they immediately choked to death. The guests began lamenting, "It's terrible. Terrible." They asked Rabbi Yitzhak Luria, "Why them? They're such holy people."

He said, "In their previous lives, they had made everything holy, except food. So when they started their new life together and looked at the food, they agreed from now on that would be holy also. The moment they opened their mouths to eat, God took them. He plucked them at their moment of highest perfection."

From that point of view, there is no tragedy left. But for us, there is the issue of tragedy. In Auschwitz, there is a room with a big display case of childrens' and babies' shoes. It is very sad to see. Almost a million children were killed by the Nazis in eastern Europe. So all the nice things we say: "They came down for a little while," "They completed their trip," falls short at this point. The element of the tragic that is involved remains.

The plane on which we find ourselves has this tragedy built in. The universe is not so just.

In relating to parents who have lost a child it is good to enlarge their scope, their imagination. Stories like the ones I've mentioned have the ability to do this. We have no way of knowing whether they are true or not, but when a person has a certain insight, they feel as if they're true.

A woman went to the Prophet Elijah. She said, "Holy Prophet, my baby has died. You have brought so many children down, what can you do for him?" He said, "Bring me two eggs and I can make the baby live again." The woman said, "Good, I'll bring them quickly." "Don't forget," he said. "In order for the eggs to work, they must come from a home where there is no bereavement."

The woman knocked on every door in the whole *shtetl*. Everyone was willing to give her eggs, but in every case, there had been bereavement. So she went back to Elijah and said, "I understand."

People who reinforce the "victim-ness" of the bereaved parents are running into trouble and they will give them trouble, too. The point is, we have to let go.

The best thing is to work it through with the parents, acknowledging that there is a tragedy, that it happened. That's the way nature works out its balances. If God is willing to trust nature, I think we should be willing to trust nature, too.

Zalman Meshullam Schachter, born in Zolkiew, Poland, was ordained as a rabbi in June, 1947. He is an author; has served as a facilitator at Esalen; and has taught at the University of California at Santa Cruz, Naropa Institute, the Lama Foundation, and the Pacific School of Religion. He is a founding faculty member of Havurat Sholom Seminary in Boston, was head of the Department of Near Eastern and Judaic Studies at the University of Manitoba, and is Professor of Religion in Jewish Mysticism at Temple University.

# 7

# *Support Groups and Organizations*

This is a sampling of the support groups and organizations available in the United States and Canada for parents of children who have died. It is likely that by contacting one of these organizations you will be led to a support group nearer to where you live.

## *Hanuman Foundation Dying Project*

"The goal is ultimately creating a space, physical or otherwise, in which people can use death as a vehicle for awakening. That is something that is familiar in other traditions, though not so familiar in the West. Most of the work that is being done with death in America, the 'new look' in dying, is toward making it psychologically comfortable, and that has to be done; that's the beginning of the whole process. But out of, say, every thousand people that die maybe one really wants to awaken. And they would like to use their experience, whether it be life or death, as a vehicle for awakening. But it's hard to do that when you're surrounded by people who are asleep into the issue of death because of their fear or self-oriented kindness or whatever. Wouldn't it be wonderful to be surrounded by beings who are interested in using *your* death to awaken them while you're using it to awaken as well? You might, at the moment of death, pass with moment-to-moment awareness from the arms of love into love itself.'

The Hanuman Foundation Dying Project provides retreats, lectures, tapes, and written material for the dying and those related to them.

The Hanuman Foundation's address is P.O. Box 2228, Taos, New Mexico 87571, (505) 983-2775.

## *Shanti Nilaya*

"When you look back at the anguish, suffering, and traumas in your life, you'll see that these are the periods of biggest growth. After a loss that brings you dreadfully painful months, you are a different man, a different woman. Many years later, they will be able to look back and see the positive things—togetherness in their family, faith or whatever—that came out of their pain " (Elisabeth Kübler-Ross).

Shanti Nilaya, sanskrit for "Home of Peace," was founded in Escondido, California in 1976 by Elisabeth Kübler-Ross. It is a nonprofit organization whose purpose is to encourage people to view life not as a threatening and painful ordeal, but as a series of challenging experiences from birth through death. It offers workshops and seminars for bereaved families (parents of murdered children and suicides, and those who lost children by illness and accidents), as well as those who have to finish unfinished business before tragedy strikes.

Shanti Nilaya's address is P.O. Box 2396, Escondido, California 92025, (714) 749-2008.

## *Compassionate Friends*

"Being at Compassionate Friends makes you feel you're talking to someone who knows exactly what you're talking about.

"We get a lot of calls from people who've lost their children. We have a woman in our group who's come to our meetings for two years. Though she says very little, you can tell it's a real support for her here. You don't have to be any particular way at our meetings. Whatever way you are is fine."

Compassionate Friends is a nondenominational self-help organization open to parents who have experienced the death of a child.

The first Compassionate Friends was founded by the Reverend Simon Stephens and a group of bereaved parents in Coventry, England, who discovered their grief was lessened by sharing it with one another.

After growing throughout the United Kingdom, the organization branched out, arriving in the United States in 1972. Their aims are:

- To offer support and friendship to any sorrowing parent;
- To listen with understanding and provide "telephone friends" who may be called;

• To provide monthly sharing groups;

• To give cognitive information about the grieving process through programs and library;

• To provide an interaction between the newly bereaved and parents whose "sorrow has softened and who have found fresh hope and strength for living."

The address of the national headquarters of Compassionate Friends in the United States is P.O. Box 1347, Oak Brook, Illinois 60521, (312) 323-5010.

The Canadian headquarters of the Compassionate Friends is 521 Montrose Street, Winnipeg, Manitoba, R3M 3M3.

## *The Center for Death Education and Research*

"To acknowledge a death is to recognize a life. In a society where there is a strong tendency for many to respond to the death of another by turning away, the recognition and acceptance of a death ultimately proclaims a personal identity for self. In this regard, the caregiver, whether doctor, nurse, clergyman, funeral director, or friend, has an important role to play in assuring that the response to a death is a life-confirming event."

The Center for Death Education and Research was established at the University of Minnesota in July 1969. Its objective is to bring recent and relevant ideas, information, and insights concerning the subject of death to as wide an audience as possible.

It has sponsored symposia on various aspects of death, grief, and bereavement, been involved in community outreach programs, presented TV programs on the sociology of death over public broadcasting channels, offered classes at both the graduate and undergraduate levels; supported research projects exploring questions regarding death and dying; and established a cassette tape library of lectures, interviews, and panel discussions on death-related topics.

The address is Center for Death Education and Research, 1167 Social Sciences Building, University of Minnesota, Minneapolis, Minnesota 55455, (612) 376-3641 or (612) 373-3683.

## *The Shanti Project*

"Here at the Shanti Project, we are committed to a vision, one in which no one, except by choice, dies alone or has to grieve without emotional support. Eventually, of course, we would hope for the kind of community awareness that would make the work of our project unnecessary."

The Shanti Project, whose volunteer grief counselors range in age from 21 to 82, provides free counseling for dying people and the bereaved. They also offer support and training for professionals working with the dying, i.e. nurses, clergy, and tutors. They also have a speaker's bureau.

"We began with fourteen volunteers and an answering machine. Our idea was to match clients in need with volunteers who wanted to help and who had gotten past their own fears about death. We looked for volunteers with a high tolerance of role ambiguity; who had a profound respect for people's processes and self-confidence and insight. We wanted to make sure they weren't going into this work for self-aggrandizement, but because they genuinely wanted to make a contribution.

"We found we tapped a well of altruism in offering our volunteers a chance to be unselfish in a way people don't normally get to be in this society. We also offered them an opportunity to be intimate with people in a very deep way."

The address of the Shanti Project is 1314 Addison Street, Berkeley, California 94609, (415) 849-4980.

## *The Grief Education Institute*

"Understanding grief and mourning can begin, like sex education, with young children, and proceed for the rest of our lives. The capacity to grieve and mourn successfully can often lead to significant freedom and growth. If we can learn to mourn well, and help others to do the same, our lives and deaths will be immeasurably enriched" (John S. Graves, M.D.).

The Grief Education Institute is a nonprofit organization whose programs include workshops, seminars, and lectures throughout the state of Colorado. Each workshop and program is designed to meet the specific needs of the group requesting the services, and is created to help individuals deal in a more healthy manner with their own death-related grief and to be more effective in helping others deal with grief.

GEI also provides telephone counseling; support groups for the bereaved; public educational programs; educational programs for professionals; a lending library;

a quarterly newsletter; and a referral to other community resources.

The address is P.O. Box 623, Englewood, Colorado 80151, (303) 777-9234.

## *St. Francis Center*

The St. Francis Center is a nonprofit organization whose purpose is to counsel and assist individuals and families facing life-threatening illness or loss and to educate the general public regarding death and dying to promulgate the concept that the quality of death is integral to the quality of life.

Their services include seminars, workshops, and trainings regarding various aspects of death and dying.

The address is St. Francis Center, 1768 Church Street N.W., Washington, D.C. 20036, (202) 234-5613.

## *S.A.N.D. and H.A.N.D.*

"People view miscarriages, abortions, and stillbirths very lightly, as if the parents shouldn't be upset. The parents themselves don't know they have the right to feel the way they feel. Instead we hear women say things like: 'I don't know why I feel so upset; I never even felt the baby move.' "

S.A.N.D. (Support After Neonatal Death) was started by Janet Kirksey and Marty Enriquez at Berkeley's Alta Bates Hospital.

"This hospital has a high-risk obstetrics program, so we see a lot of fetal and neonatal deaths here. I thought we did a good job when we were on duty but when one of us wasn't here and someone's baby died, there were a lot of people we missed. I read an article on H.A.N.D. (Helping After Neonatal Death), an organization in Marin County, and began referring patients there. They asked why I didn't start a group here. Our program is open to people from hospitals all over the East Bay. We provide a support group, consulting, and educational services to parents who've gone through a neonatal death."

S.A.N.D., Alta Bates Hospital, 3001 Colby Street at Ashby, Berkeley, California 94705, (415) 845-7110.

H.A.N.D., P.O. Box 62, San Anselmo, California 94960. (No telephone listing.)

## *Nautilus*

"Just as the Nautilus shell suggests, the organization represents the multi-chambered growth of our lives in the different phases and levels of the physical and spiritual."

Nautilus is a non-profit organization which provides grief counseling.

NAUTILUS, c/o Anthropos Foundation, 1826 Catalina Court, Livermore, California 94550, (415) 447-2277.

## *Hospices*

A hospice is defined as an alternative form of providing services to the terminally ill and their families. In the

United States, the National Hospice Organization was established to inform interested parties of the growth and direction of the increasing number of hospice care institutions, to assist all the hospice groups nationwide to work together to affect various federal laws, to develop and implement standards for hospices, to carry on educational programs, to publish information on hospice activities, to hold symposiums, and to put out a hospice journal.

The agreed-upon goals of many hospices within this organization are as follows:

- The terminally ill person will be able to live as fully and completely as possible, free of pain, with medication before the need is felt.
- The entire family is considered the unit of care, rather than just the patient.
- The hospice is to supplement existing community services.
- The hospice will be available to educate health care professionals and the public.

A directory of hospices may be obtained by writing to the National Hospice Organization, 765 Prospect Street, New Haven, Connecticut 06511, (203) 787-5871.

# 8

My own after-death experience of my child occurred a number of years after she died. I had been taking part in a very intensive training with a support group which lasted for six days. Before going, I assumed I would have numerous realizations but hadn't counted on having my relationship to Gabrielle's death being an issue. As it turned out, a great portion of the workshop revolved around this, although I had imagined this part of my life to be finished. I hadn't experienced anger or sadness about it for at least two years and I could quite rationally discuss the entire subject. Except for one thing. In order to accommodate the doctor of my choice—so that the baby could be born at his office, rather than in a hospital—I had labor induced. This was not in keeping with my own values regarding health and "having things happen at the right time." However, I suppressed such thoughts and entered into the event willingly.

After Gabrielle was born dead, I was afraid that what

killed her during labor was the fact labor was induced. My doctor, going through his own anguish, assured me that this was highly unlikely. I bought that line of reasoning, mainly because the experience of that guilt appeared so painful I was afraid it would kill me if I unleashed it. I also feared people would think I was a murderer if they knew I had had the birth induced.

During my workshop, I told the entire group about this. The man leading the training asked if I were willing to forgive myself for this and, after examining this question, I knew I wasn't. He then asked if I were willing to ask Gabrielle for her forgiveness. A novel idea. When I looked within myself to ask this question, I could find neither hide nor hair of Gabrielle. She simply was not a part of my experience.

After that evening's session, I went back to my room and found I was unable to sleep or think about anything else but my relationship with Gabrielle. It was very late and everyone else was asleep in bed. I sat up on the living room floor and what began to emerge was a rush of thoughts and emotions and physical sensations associated with her death—loss, sorrow, guilt, anger. They came tumbling out. I rapidly entered into each one, knowing I couldn't avoid any of it if I wanted to eventually reach Gabrielle. Nor did I know where this tack was leading. I sat on the floor until morning, knowing, fearing the process was hopeless and would go on forever and lead to nothing.

As the sun came up through the window, however, all of a sudden, there was Gabrielle. It was not an image I



CAMBRIA COUNTY LIBRARY
JOHNSTOWN, PA. 15901

was seeing outside myself. It was more akin to a mental image. It certainly wasn't the type of picture I usually assembled—rather, it came spontaneously. And it wasn't an image of a baby but of a young woman. I started to cry. Her first words were, "Are you still crying about that, mother?"

I said, "Yes. I just want to know if you forgive me."

Her reply was, "I never didn't forgive you. That's just the way it was."

I asked, "Will you always be here?"

She said, "I've always been here."

"I love you," I said.

"I love you, too," she said.

I can only say that that interchange completed the experience of my daughter's death for me and that, after having had a dead child, she was now alive for me again.

It may be that your interpretation of this experience is that the incident was one of making myself feel better, of mental manipulation or imagination. For me, what occurred was a shift in the manner in which I related to Gabrielle's death. It became something that had happened, rather than a tragedy. It became appropriate.

"Birth is not a beginning; death is not an end."

—Chuang-tzu

NO LONGER PROPERTY
OF CAMBRIA CO LIBRARY

AUG 19

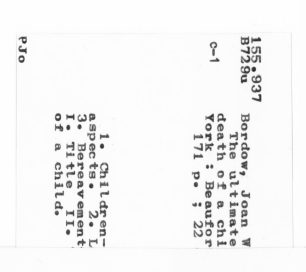

155.937
B729u
C-1
Bordow, Joan W
The ultimate
death of a chi
York : Beaufor
171 p. ; 22

1. Children-
aspects. 2. L
3. Bereavement
I. Title II.
of a child.

PJo

155.937
B729u
c-1

Bordow, Joan Wiener, 1944-
The ultimate loss : coping with the death of a child / Joan Bordow. -- New York : Beaufort Books, [c1982]
171 p. ; 22 cm.

CAMBRIA COUNTY LIBRARY
Johnstown, PA 15901

FINES: PER DAY
Adults 10¢, Children 5¢

1. Children--Death--Psychological aspects. 2. Loss (Psychology) 3. Bereavement--Psychological aspects. I. Title II. Title: Surviving the deat of a child.

PJo JOCCxc 81-1818